The Shoestring Girl

OTHER TITLES BY ANNIE JEAN BREWER

Nonfiction Titles

The Minimalist Cleaning Method

How to Start Out or Over on a Shoestring

400 Ways to Save a Fortune

How to Write and Sell an Ebook

How to Write Ebooks For a Living

Where to Work Online

Professional Help: How to Prevent and Fix Malware, Viruses, Spyware and Other Baddies

How to Watch Stuff Online For Free

Be Happy Now

How to Be Happy

Fiction Titles

163 Nights

The Bean Pot and Other Tales

What About Bob?

THE SHOESTRING GIRL: HOW I LIVE ON PRACTICALLY NOTHING AND YOU CAN TOO!

ANNIE BREWER

First published in ebook format worldwide in 2011

By Annie Jean Brewer

www.annienygma.com

FIRST PRINT EDITION

Copyright 2012 by Annie Jean Brewer

PUBLISHED BY:

Annie Jean Brewer on CreateSpace

For Katie

TABLE OF CONTENTS

THE SHOESTRING
GIRL

INTRODUCTION

When I left my husband a decade ago I had no job and no money; all I had were my kids, our pets and an old mobile home that I had purchased in preparation.

I did not enter into the challenge without being ready. I knew my income would be sparse so I planned ahead. These were my rules:

- Make recurring expenses as low as they could go.
- Keep them that way.

By using this method I would know the bare minimum needed to survive with my kids and I could (hopefully) be a little picky and choose a job that offered mother's hours so I would not have to depend upon child care for all but the youngest.

It worked.

When my income increased I followed the advice of some friends and took out loans and credit cards to "improve my situation" with new appliances and furniture. What a mistake! As a result of those purchases there were a few times when I had to scrape money together just to buy groceries.

I don't want to EVER do that again.

I have discovered several advantages to keeping those recurring expenses low:

- It frees up the bulk of your money for enjoying life.
- You don't have to work as hard to get your bills paid.
- You can better survive economic downturns.
- You can afford to chase your dreams or take risks.
- You can afford to take long vacations by saving up and not working for a time.
- You don't have to search for a roommate or shack up with someone to have help paying your bills--you are able to pay all of your bills on a single income.

I have been living this lifestyle for so many years now that it is second nature. I have become the one that my wealthier friends ask for loans when their income takes a dip. It makes me wonder who is the truly wealthy one: the one with all of the money, or the one who knows how to keep it?

Some say that this lifestyle involves sacrifice yet neither I nor my family feels this way. We do what we want, when we want and have money to spare.

Our van is paid for, we rent a nice older home in town and we have money in the bank with more on the way. Our computers are newer (Katie's is 2 years old and mine is a few months old) and we can afford to upgrade on a regular cycle.

We have everything we need but only a portion of the expense of an average household. Here are my recurring bills:

Rent	$250.00
Water/Sewage/Trash	$35
Internet	$30
Car Insurance	$41.00 ($245 every 6 months)
Home Phone	$1.67 ($20/year)
Electric	$45.00
Total:	**$402.67/month**

Up until recently I had a part-time job at Wal-Mart. We have enough money coming in from my book royalties so I quit to focus on the things that are really important in my life. This accomplishment would have been impossible if it were not for shoestring living.

We did have prepaid cell phones but stopped putting money on them when I started planning to leave the job at Wal-Mart. Cell phones are luxuries for all but the perpetually mobile (like truck drivers) so instead we use Google Voice combined with our MagicJack for voice calls and texting.

We do not receive welfare or food stamps yet we eat well and are healthy. Nor do we receive any cash payments from the government. We live entirely on my income as a writer and life is really good.

If we wanted to, we could live on even less than we do right now. Here's how:

- Go to the library for internet access. Save $30/month.
- Eliminate the van and walk everywhere. Save $41/month on car insurance plus maintenance, gasoline, taxes and license fees. Realistic savings would be over $1,000 a year.
- Use Google Voice exclusively for phone service instead of MagicJack. Save $1.67/month
- Purchase a mobile home on a rented lot and pay cash. Save $100-$150 a month depending upon the lot rent.

If I did these things I would then only pay $230 a month for an additional savings of $202.67. If I wanted to live even cheaper I could purchase a small RV or live in my van and eliminate the rental and utility fees so even *my* low bills are not the lowest that they could be!

However there is a line we must walk when being frugal. The goal is to stay on the comfortable side of that line so that our lives do not feel like a sacrifice. Rather like walking on a tightrope, we balance to avoid a fall. I call this line the shoestring.

Anyone can do what I do to save money. All it takes is desire, patience and a willingness to look at things in a different way.

Are you ready to live on a shoestring?

How to Use This Book

Within these pages you will find the tips and tricks that I have used personally over the years to pare my expenses to the bone. Some of these things I still do today while others did not hold my interest; still others I've kept in reserve for the day that I need the knowledge.

This book is written so that you can read it in its entirety to get an overview and then bookmark the stuff you want to try yourself. I have no intentions of reinventing the wheel so if there is a resource available that can help you better I will lead you there with a link or a reference. That way if you want to know more you can find it but if not you can just skip over. I have done this deliberately to save you time while you learn about saving money.

If you don't like an idea, that's okay. Just move to the next one. The frugality police are not going to knock on your door just because you use paper products or enjoy eating out!

Above all have fun while you experiment. If you try something and don't enjoy it then put it back on the shelf and try something else. The object of the game is to keep trying and experimenting--to keep thinking out of the box that you are trapped in.

If any of these ideas make you think then I have done my job. If you know of any ideas that will make this book better, email me your suggestions at annie@annienygma.com..

Thank you for your support!

DISCLAIMER

As with any book we have to have a section with the legal stuff. I am not your mother and there isn't any warranty implied or implicated in any form in any of these pages. I am not responsible for any loss, dismemberment or jail time you incur because you tried the stuff in this book. Use your brain and check your local laws. I use this stuff but you may not want to take the risk.

A TEMPORARY SITUATION

Ideally, living on a shoestring should be a temporary situation for most of the folks who try it. Once your expenses are as low as they can go you will have the free time to pursue other forms of income.

For instance, you can share your tips and tricks on living frugally in a simple book[1] like this one to generate income even while you sleep. Everyone is special and has knowledge to share; not enough of us realize that we each have something important to contribute to the world.

If you are not interested in sharing your knowledge there are other ways of creating income, both passive and regular. Two books I recommend for those who are sincerely interested in improving their financial situation are The Millionaire Fastlane by MJ DeMarco and Where to Work Online[2] (written by me).

I used my shoestring skills to be a stay at home mother for my daughter while she was younger; now I use those same skills to pursue my love of writing and help others through my books. Sometimes I even take a

---

[1] For more information read How to Write and Sell an Ebook by Annie Brewer
http://www.smashwords.com/books/view/36647
[2] http://www.smashwords.com/books/view/36433

break and stop working entirely - an extended stay at home vacation that is paid for with the money I've saved. The possibilities are endless once you live beneath your means!

Be warned that the shoestring lifestyle can be addictive: once you discover how little it actually can take to live well you may not want to go back to your old life even if you're rolling in the dough!

WELFARE, SOCIAL SECURITY AND JOBS

My belief in Social Security went out the door along with the Easter Bunny and Santa Claus. Here is a person who shares my opinion:

http://www.cnn.com/2011/09/20/opinion/granderson-social-security/index.html?hpt=hp_c2

True, there are many who have figured out how to game the system; who get "disability," food stamps, medical assistance, utility assistance and however many other "assistances" that are out there but I don't.

It isn't that I think they are wrong; I simply do not trust that money to be there should I ever *really* need it so I do not want to grow dependent.

As a result I am planning for a future without government assistance: along with saving some money I am building passive income. Eventually should I settle down I may invest in cheap mobile homes to rent for extra money as well. An apartment building, where the owner lives in one unit and rents out the others has been an investment I have also considered.

Or perhaps I will continue to live on practically nothing.

One day the government's money will dry up. It has to. Logic dictates that nothing can continue to spend more than it receives without eventually hitting a wall. All of us have a credit limit. When our nation reaches that limit austerity measures will be taken in a last ditch attempt to keep the government afloat.

Payment to the states for food, medical benefits, SSI, disability payments and other monies to the defenseless will be the first to go.

Benefits to the retirees will be next. Some of them actually have money to fight so I don't expect them to be in the first wave.

When that happens watch to see what happens when millions who have not learned to count upon themselves discover that they've traveled up the Shit Creek and just lost their only paddle.

I have no intention of being one of those people. I plan to be on the sidelines watching, safely away from the shit that will hit the fan.

I will be one of the several who will actually be able to survive--thrive even--without government assistance.

"But what about a regular job?"

Regular jobs are nice if you don't count on them. This economy has shown that we are unable to count upon those jobs to be there when we need them.

For instance, Wal-Mart is one of the biggest employers in the United States. Millions of people work there every day. Students, singles, fathers, mothers, retirees all work for this mecca of consumerism.

While I worked there the past several weeks saw a slow reduction in our hours without a single explanation. Currently a large number of my fellow part time workers have watched their hours reduced to 16 hours a week. They even expected me to drive from a neighboring town for 4 hours a day.

Note: I love Wal-Mart even if I don't agree with all of their practices. They're one of the cheapest places around for shoestringers to get what they need.

A friend in a nearby department hired on to join the management program. He is living with his parents because he could not afford to support his children on the 30-plus part time hours a week he originally received. When he confronted his supervisor about his drastically reduced hours he was informed that he would have to deal with it because he was "low head on the totem pole."

Another young lady, a single mother, is a cashier at the very same store. She burst out in tears when she saw her 16 work-hour schedule. She, like me, is all alone in the duties of supporting her children. She has no clue how she will pay her bills or how long she will last.

Another gentleman had a conniption when he discovered his hours; his wife is the primary breadwinner and is currently laid up from a surgery - he has no idea how he will make ends meet while she is off work.

The tension there was so thick that you could feel it when you walked through the halls. The managers cringed when they asked you how you were doing, waiting to get pounced upon by angry employees.

This is what corporate security will get you: a bunch of empty promises. Almost every place of employment can be counted on to consider their workers "lucky" to have a job and will treat them as such. In some places you are lucky to even get a break. I've worked in a number of restaurants where I had to pretend to take up cigarette smoking in order to get a "smoke" break -- the smokers frequently relaxed outside while the nonsmokers were expected to take up the slack without complaint.

Businesses will promise you the moon and then cut your hours at the slightest provocation; I knew one manager whose favorite punishment was not scheduling workers who fell out of favor, sometimes for weeks at a time. These workers would be so happy to be allowed to work again they would fall under her thumb and gratefully do whatever she asked.

Others would regularly lay off people -- sometimes weekly. Your days would be spent in terror of attracting unwanted notice, terrified that you would be called into the office or taken for a walk. When they didn't lay off you were forced to work for 50-60 hours a week in wintertime: 10 hours a day with "encouragement" to work all of them and sometimes they would even work up to 70 by opening the factory all seven days of the week. Those who worked like slaves in the winter were the ones who generally escaped the layoffs in the summer.

Some will promise you the moon - and lay you off before the next one. Still others refuse to lay people off and instead fire their workers for the smallest offense and refuse to pay unemployment.

When you get closer to retirement age a reason will be found to fill your spot with someone younger to avoid the promised stipend; sometimes the fortunate ones can sue and get a portion back but most just feel powerless and move on to their next career as a greeter at Wal-Mart.

Job security is NO security. It is simply a bunch of empty promises issued to keep the masses docile. The only real security to be had in this country is by those who count upon themselves.

Is this what you want for your future?

If not then the time to act is now. Start by reducing your expenses to the bare minimum while creating sources of income that are not dependent upon a public job. Small businesses do not need a lot of capital to start. A few tools, an ad in a paper, maybe some free business cards from Vistaprint and you are on your way.

Instead of being dependent upon one source of income you will have lots of little sources. If one client stops using you there will be others to take his place.

Look for ways to make your money take care of you. Buy an inexpensive mobile home and rent it out for additional income. Take that income and buy another one, Repeat. Buy a duplex and rent out one side to pay the expenses. You will have a home rent-free then.

Start working online[3] and stash the cash to invest in something else. Grow a garden and sell the produce. Heck, sell your junk on eBay or Craigslist!

The sooner you work to reduce your expenses and diversify your income the sooner you will gain real security. I know from experience that most employers will treat you like garbage if they know they are your only source of money. If they know that you have enough income from other sources to walk away--and the guts to do so if they pull any crap--they will treat you with much more respect.

Now, are you ready for true job security, or are you content with a cheap imitation?

---

[3] Where to Work Online by Annie Brewer
http://www.smashwords.com/books/view/36433

LIVE ON LESS

One thing I have learned over the years is that we all have the ability to live on much less than we think we can. The amazing part is that living on less will not make you feel deprived but instead you will feel liberated if it is done in a rational manner.

There are numerous reasons to live on less:

- **It is cheaper**. It is much cheaper not to buy something than to buy it, bring it home and care for it.
- **It saves time**. It takes less time not to buy something than it does to buy it and care for it.
- Less to clean.
- Less to care for.
- Less to store.
- Less to move.
- Less to trip over.

There is **a trick to living with less** and it does NOT involve going cold turkey. The trick is to **start small**.

- When you feel the desire to acquire something, ask yourself if you have something else already that will accomplish the job.
- If it is a decorative item imagine it dusty and dirty or tossed in a box stuffed in a storage

cubby somewhere. You can also imagine it with a 10-cent price tag stuck to it. If it is solely decorative why are you even considering it anyway?

I put a moratorium on acquisitions I while I slowly started eliminating things that did NOT get used. If I had 20 knives but only used 5 regularly, 15 were purged. The same went for clothing and everything else I owned.

Just putting a halt to extraneous purchases has saved me thousands of dollars and when combined with networking I have saved thousands more.

There are tons of decluttering websites so I won't reinvent the wheel. Just know that less stuff can bring you more time and more secure finances.

If you want to see a list of the bare minimum items you need to start out, start over or just get buy check out my book How to Start Out or Over on a Shoestring[4]. That will give you an idea of how low you can REALLY go. I started out with even less than what is in the book when I moved here.

The majority of the information you will find available these days concerns the active saving of money. These methods include clipping coupons, switching to

---

[4] http://www.smashwords.com/books/view/69709

generic brands, buying in bulk, watching for sales and thrifting but there is one form of frugality that is being given short shrift when in fact it is the most frugal of all the methods described. This method alone has saved me a fortune over the years and continues to save me even now.

The Ultimate Frugality is to Stop Buying and Using.

- Instead of trying to secure the best deal on a new pair of pants wear the ones you have and leave the new ones in the store.
- Instead of shopping and scouting for a dryer, string a line and hang your clothes out to dry.
- Instead of using a dishwasher wash your dishes by hand and sell that machine for scrap.
- Instead of driving a car you can walk, ride a bike or use public transportation.
- Instead of leaving things on turn everything off when you aren't using them or don't use certain things at all. This goes for water and other utilities as well to help save on those bills.

SOMETHING TO CONSIDER

While it is impossible to stop buying entirely consider the fact that not purchasing something will save you more time, trouble and expense than shopping for the best deal.

- Instead of buying paper towels wash and reuse those cloth ones you have decorating your refrigerator.
- Instead of buying bathroom tissue give that mountain of wash cloths an extra use.
- Instead of buying the latest and greatest spray cleaner spritz that mess with the vinegar you already have in your pantry.

This is more than *"use it up, wear it out."* This is about refusing to bow to the artificial needs created by advertising.

How many shirts can you wear at one time? If you wore a different shirt every single day how many weeks would it take for you to work through every shirt in your closet? If you have so many shirts already do you really need another one? Do you think that a new shirt will make you prettier or more successful? Acknowledge the real reason for wanting to buy that item and fix the reason instead of throwing money away on an empty purchase.

There is a term for the hard-core no-buy-it frugalists; they are called Minimalists. Minimalists have realized that it is not just enough to simply hunt out the best bargains but to minimize what they buy, period. Some of these extremists own less than 100 things total. Imagine how little you would have to spend if all you needed were 100 things!

Imagine how easy it would be to pack or to move to a different home. Imagine life without storage bills or tripping over piles of stuff.

I'm not asking you to do it, just to consider the possibility.

Consider the possibility that there are things in your life you don't have to buy and just imagine what life would be like with a little less stuff in your shopping cart. Then imagine how much thicker your wallet would be if you made that one simple change.

Just imagine.

THE CURSE OF CREDIT

T here is no other way to say this:

You don't need credit.

Period.

If you can't afford to pay for it when you get it you don't need it.

Do you have any clue what you are doing when you sign up for those credit cards or those car loans?

You are signing away your future; giving away days and weeks and possibly YEARS of your life to enjoy something that will be long gone before you even finish paying for it!

Are you a fortune teller? Can you absolutely positively GUARANTEE that you won't be laid off, fired or injured before the day is over? Can you foresee if there is a tornado, landslide, earthquake, flood or other disaster on the way?

You can't?

Neither can I.

That is why you need to avoid credit like the plague. You don't know what is going to happen in your future any more than any of us do.

Those credit notes are a prediction that NOTHING is going to happen to your income in the future and that you will have more than enough money to pay. Can you honestly guarantee that?

Look at it this way: Could you afford to lose your car tomorrow? What about your house?

No? You could lose them easily if the bank decided to repossess.

If you can't afford to lose it then you need to own it free and clear. You cannot take a short cut on this.

RENT TO OWN

Once upon a time I was young and considered sexy. It was during this time that the district manager of a very popular rent to own chain insisted upon taking me to dinner.

He spent the evening showing me how much money he made and was happy to oblige my curiosity about his work. He bragged that every single item is priced so that they earn back the purchase price in 4-6 months. Research had been done that demonstrated that the average renter only keeps items for that period of time and the odds of it being damaged were high. If a renter keeps an item past that point the money they spend past that 4-6 month span is pure profit.

This is the primary reason rent to own places work so hard to suck you in--they are making a fortune. For instance, a friend of mine was purchasing a big-screen television from the local rental place. After making the payments for a year he decided he wanted to pay it off. He was informed that his payoff was still over a thousand dollars! He went to Sears and purchased a brand new, even bigger television for $750 and let the rented one go back.

If you have an item that you are renting to own, how much is your payoff? Could you take that money and purchase an entirely new item instead?

SIGNIFICANT SAVINGS

When you stop buying things on credit you will end up saving a fortune. The simplest of car purchases on credit can cost thousands of dollars in interest; a number of credit cards charge a minimum $5 in finance fees every month. We won't even discuss how many YEARS you can pay on a house before you even start paying on the principal.

Start looking at your statements. Call your creditors and ask how much interest you have paid in the past couple of months.

Go ahead, ask them. I'll wait.

Annie Brewer

Imagine what you could have done if you weren't wasting all of that money.

THE LUXURY OF INSURANCE

I don't have any insurance that I am not legally required to own. Neither medical nor life insurance policies are in my portfolio.

When I revealed that fact on my blog[5] there was some consternation among my readers: "What if something bad happens?"

In my opinion, having insurance is like paying a bookie.

"Hey Moe, I'll bet you that I won't get cancer or somethin' while I have your policy but if I get it, you gotta pay for it!"

Moe looks up from the money he's counting and takes the cigar out of his mouth. "Yeah, I'll take that bet! Chances are ya won't get it anyway. I want $$$ every month to take that bet!"

Guess who is winning?

Let's be honest: if something drastic were to happen like an accident or an illness your finances will be trashed regardless. That is just how life is in this country. It doesn't matter if you have paid millions out in insurance, you will be screwed if only because you are no longer able to work.

---

[5] You can find my blog at www.annienygma.com.

You are damned if you do and damned if you don't. Since the result is the same either way why not take your chances and save your money?

If you are concerned place what you would put in a premium into a special interest-bearing account. For most of you, just looking over how much you spent in insurance premiums minus what you would have paid in medical expenses is enough to show you the light.

Of course it is different if you have a number of health issues already; this is for those who are relatively healthy right now and plan to take the steps to remain healthy in the future. Don't drop it if you actually need and use it.

THE PENNY TRAP

While you are exploring the shoestring lifestyle take care not to fall into the Penny Trap. The Penny Trap is where we spend all of our time saving pennies while neglecting the big issues that are leaking huge dollars from our wallets.

For instance, I know a person who leases a new car every year but insists upon using tea bags three and four times before throwing them away.

I know another who will drive miles for a sale and put all of the purchases on high-interest credit cards.

How about the family who refuses to buy garbage bags but owns a house so big they never use some of the rooms?

Or the person that eats off of the Dollar Menu every day to save money?

There are as many different ways to fall into the Penny Trap as there are people in this world. The trap is so easy to fall into; I've had to climb out of it a few times myself. The only way to truly avoid falling into this trap is to completely evaluate your life and finances on occasion. Look at everything and see just exactly where your money is going.

Perhaps you subscribe to a certain cable package just to watch a single show. Could you find that one show online and eliminate all of those channels that you don't use?

Do you spend $5 in gas going to a certain store just so you can save $1 on toothpaste?

Evaluating your expenses can end up saving you a fortune; when I had credit cards it wasn't until I examined the bills that I discovered that I was paying almost $30 a month in interest fees alone. When it dawned on me that I was spending the equivalent of my Internet bill every single month just to have those stupid pieces of plastic I cancelled them. I would have never known had I not decided to re-evaluate my financial life and stop just paying the bills blindly.

We all have these leaks that we can't see because we are focused on stopping the tiny trickles. Take care of the big breaks and the little trickles will take care of themselves.

Some things may seem thrifty but actually waste more time, resources, energy and even money than if you did without. These things are considered to be **hard thrift**.

For instance, instead of saving toilet paper rolls to stash your power cords in, wrap those cords upon themselves to store them without the cardboard rolls. Use your hand or elbow (depending upon the length of cord) to wrap the cord around. Leave a foot or so free from the plug.

Remove the cord from your hand and use the remaining length to wrap around the center of the cord to make the cord look like a bow. Don't wrap too tight-- use just enough tension to secure without stretching. Tuck the plug end of the cord through one of the bow loops and adjust. This will allow the cord to secure itself. Here is a video demonstrating how it is done:

http://www.youtube.com/watch?v=FjmLTWoB8as

Instead of using plate covers, paper towels and similar items in the microwave to avoid splashes just wipe out the microwave every time. You won't have extra items cluttering up your home and your microwave will be cleaner and more sanitary.

If you don't eat leftovers don't save them. It is a waste of time, space and food. Just cook what you expect to eat during that single meal and be done with it. I have tried this both ways and it is definitely more frugal to only cook what you will eat if the leftovers constantly go bad in your refrigerator.

Don't get stupid in an attempt to save money. For instance, if you actually use a refrigerator, buy a darn refrigerator. You don't have to get a big one but don't deprive yourself just to save a few bucks. If you like hot water don't keep the water heater shut off so that you can shiver every time you wash your hands. You will end up washing your hands less and getting sick as a result. Doctors and prescriptions are MUCH more expensive than a little hot water.

Things like this will make you miserable and end up costing more money than you save.

Don't spend $$ just to save a few pennies. Driving across town just to save fifteen cents on a bar of soap is not frugal, it is stupid. You spend more in fuel than you could possibly save, not including the time you wasted. Once when I ran a small lighting store a lady came in who insisted that we sell her a particular light for a quarter less than we had it listed because another store listed it at that price. I was unable to grant her request so she left, drove immediately to the store in question (about an hour away), purchased the light and returned to show us how she saved a quarter! When I asked her how much she spent on gas to save that twenty-five cents she huffed and left the building. Don't be stupid, people.

Factor in your time when calculating money saved. It is not a good deal to spend an hour or so doing something that will only save you a few cents. Unless you have more time than money (and even then) just spend the darn money. Pick up a few aluminum cans to make up the cost (you will probably end up ahead this way).

Buying is not always the answer to every question. Do without instead of splurging. Substitute or otherwise make do when those random needs pop up. For instance, once every so often I have something that I would like ironed. Instead of purchasing an iron I steam out the wrinkles in the bathroom--no iron required!

Making things is not always a solution. For instance, it is currently much cheaper to buy clothing at the thrift shop than it is to buy the material and make your own clothing at home. The only exception to this rule is if you receive a bunch of fabric for free.

Don't use family cloths when you have to drag them to the laundromat to keep them clean. I personally love family cloths but you go in the hole when you factor in the cost of a laundromat.

Do not use wood to heat when you have to buy the wood. Wood heat takes a lot of work regardless of whether you buy it or cut it yourself. One major time dent of wood heat is staying up all night to keep it stoked on really cold nights to prevent you and your pipes from freezing. This is also a difficulty if you have to leave home for several hours and no one is available to keep the stove stoked while you are gone. Wood heat can be inexpensive but you will save time and money by locating another heating method for your home especially if you have to deal with frozen water pipes. At the very least have a backup heating method for when you aren't home or are asleep if you decide to use this method.

Don't grow your own "everything." Some foods like wheat take up a large amount of real estate and a huge amount of effort to harvest. It is much cheaper both time and moneywise to just buy a bag of food-grade wheat and be done with it.

I'm sure you get the idea here. The goal is to save money but **not to be stupid in the process**. I've known people who spent hundreds of dollars on equipment that only saved them a few bucks in money - or a few minutes in time. Consider your purchases, creations and thrifty methods well.

Housing

Housing is one of the major expenses of any family but there are several ways that you can pare down this expense.

Rule #1 is to **never have more house than you actually need or can use**. There are several reasons for this rule:

- The more space, the more it costs to rent/purchase.
- The more space, the more it costs to heat/cool.
- The more space, the more you have to clean/maintain.
- The more space, the more it costs to fill up with stuff like furniture.

I don't care what the "experts" say: always go on the small side when it comes to housing. The only exception to this would be if you are presented with the opportunity to purchase a home or mobile home for cash to eliminate your housing bill entirely. If that happens, buy the place and close off the rooms you don't need or fix it up and sell it at a profit to purchase a home that better fits your family.

For instance, when I first moved out I lived with my three daughters in a 10x50 mobile home. The two older girls shared the bedroom while the youngest and I slept on a futon in the living room. The mobile home was paid for so all we had to worry about was $100 lot rent every month--a significant savings over what it would have cost us to rent an apartment. Currently my youngest and I live in a 1-bedroom house we rent for $250/month. She gets the bedroom while I use a futon on the living room floor.

A few years ago my youngest and I purchased a 12x60 2-bedroom mobile home for a song. Lot rent was $100 a month there as well. We really didn't need that much space so in the winter we would close off the back bedroom to save on heating costs. It was too big for us but we saved more by living there than if we had rented something in that area better suited to the size we needed.

DO YOU HAVE TOO MUCH HOUSE?

- Do you have rooms dedicated to a special purpose, hobbies and/or storage?
- Do you have a guest room but don't entertain guests on a daily or weekly basis?
- Do you have rooms for kids that aren't even at home anymore?

If you answered "yes" to any of these questions then you have too much house. Consider downsizing until you reach the point where every room gets used daily. Why spend money on rooms that aren't used?

Shop around for the best deal on a right-sized home or apartment. Ask your friends and acquaintances about inexpensive places to rent. I located this home while walking around town one day with a friend; the tenants had vacated just days previous so I was able to secure the home before it even came on the market.

Super Cheap Housing

Inexpensive homes rarely stay empty or get advertised so networking is essential to finding the perfect inexpensive home.

The ideal house payment is none at all; taxes on a simple home will be much less than rent or a mortgage could ever be. If you have skills to fix up a place you may be able to get an abandoned home and fix it up; if you don't have the skills but are willing to learn you can check out books from the library to end up with a nice house on the cheap. Don't do this if you aren't willing to sacrifice and put in some sweat equity--older fix-it homes can require a LOT of work.

With that very serious disclaimer in mind if you are not seriously motivated to do repairs on a place (meaning you would choke if you discovered a water leak or a weak floor) you will be better off financially and emotionally to spend the extra money renting an inexpensive place and leaving the repairs to a landlord.

ADVERSE POSSESSION

A little known way to acquire a home in these challenging financial times is called adverse possession; this is a little-known law that is used to deal with abandoned homes. Check the local laws in your area covering this subject; you may be able to acquire a home for an inexpensive filing fee like a man did in Texas[6]. Visit the link in the footnote for more information.

Should I decide I want to stay in a single area this would be the one law I would check into because it can truly net you a NICE home on a shoestring, especially in this era of rampant foreclosures.

---

[6] http://www.foxnews.com/politics/2011/07/21/texas-mans-16-property-seizure-throws-obscure-law-into-spotlight/?test=latestnews

MOBILE HOMES

If you have a couple of thousand dollars saved up check Craigslist and your local classifieds (online and off) for older mobile homes for sale. I have even seen mobile homes offered for free on Freecycle. These homes are generally on a lot but if not don't bother with them unless you already have a place to move them; some lots won't accept older mobile homes. This is an excellent way to purchase a larger home if you need one. You can either stay on the lot or save up and purchase a piece of land to move your home to depending upon what your desires are.

One way to own a home and land without going into debt would be to purchase an older mobile home (make sure it is in good enough condition to move safely). Live in it and save the difference you would normally pay in rent. Purchase a lot with cash and move your mobile home there or build the home you desire while you continue to live on the rented lot. You can rent out or sell the mobile home when you no longer have any need for it.

NOTE: if you rent it out you will have an instant source of passive income. Just keep the repairs up and enjoy being able to work less. I have done this in the past and it is incredibly easy as long as you are picky about your tenants and don't get stupid with the rent you charge. I may end up doing it again if I ever land in an area where I actually want to stay.

Singles and small families can also explore larger travel trailers and fifth-wheel campers. They have just enough space, sell for reasonable amounts used and can be hooked up to standard utilities just like a regular mobile home. They also offer the advantage of being less expensive to move; instead of hiring a moving company all you have to do is rent a pickup truck with the appropriate hitch. An older couple I knew lived in a fifth-wheel camper for years and used the money they saved to live a very comfortable lifestyle with nice clothes, several vehicles and luxuries normally only afforded by those in the wealthier classes.

No "HOME" AT ALL

Some singles and couples choose to live in no home at all; instead they live in their van or RV full time. This is becoming more popular as people are forced to relocate for college or employment. To learn more about this lifestyle check out the following sites (links available in the footnotes)

- Spartan Student[7] (lived in a van while he attended college)
- Cheap RV Living[8] (covers van dwelling)
- Homeless On Wheels[9]
- We Live on a Boat[10]

You can also live in the woods but that is another subject entirely. I have neither the experience nor desire to live THAT cheap (and I doubt you do either) so I will leave that subject to the experts!

This is one of the options I am considering when my kid turns 18. I have several friends and family members who have agreed to allow me to use their back yards, farms and even driveways for extended visits so I would have no need to pay for a rental space. I can rent a Post Office box for my mail (at some remailer if not handled by a trusted confidante) and either travel or stay put as I desire. I plan to choose a smallish RV that is easily mistaken for a van in order to have maximum fuel economy and stealth for those nights I desire to park on a street corner or in a parking lot.

With the RV paid for and a solar energy system in place (or even using the onboard charging system if you move it regularly) one could have no rent at all

---

[7] http://spartanstudent.blogspot.com/

[8] http://cheaprvliving.com/

[9] http://homelessonwheels.wordpress.com/

[10] http://www.weliveonaboat.com/

using this method--sheer paradise for those tired of overbearing landlords!

Auto

I have had one vehicle in my life that required a payment. I lost that car when I became pregnant with my first child and vowed to never throw money away like that again.

As a rule I live in town so that I do not need to use a vehicle for everyday errands. Instead my daughter and I walk to the library and the local grocery. We only use the van in inclement weather, when we are hauling large things or when we have to go out of town.

If you live in a metropolitan area consider well if you even NEED a car; you can live on considerably less if you avoid this expense. There are several options available for those without a car. You can use public transportation (some small towns even have a bus-like "taxi" system), walk or invest in a scooter or moped. With a bike and a trailer you could haul your groceries and avoid a vehicle entirely. Tammy Strobel of Rowdy Kittens uses this method and wrote a book about her experience called Simply Car-Free: How to Pedal Toward Financial Freedom and a Healthier Life.

Some bike trailers can be expensive; check yard sales for parents selling the bike trailers they used with their young children. You can pick these up for a few dollars and they frequently have the added benefit of rain covers and good visibility. Who cares if you are hauling groceries instead of a kid in a trailer? I picked my trailer up for $10 and it is light enough to store in my attic when I'm not using it.

Another note on bikes: you don't need an expensive one. I bought mine from Wal-Mart several years ago when gas hit $4 a gallon. The bike cost $54 and is still going strong. Don't let yourself be ripped off - almost any old bike will get you where you need to be and anyone can do basic repairs now thanks to the copious instructions available on the Internet.

If you have a vehicle payment I encourage you to eliminate it. Pay it off, sell it--light a fire to the damn thing but get out from under that expense. You are paying hundreds if not thousands of dollars for the privilege of driving a fancy chunk of metal that drops in value every day so stop it.

A vehicle is merely a method of getting from Point A to Point B. You do not need anything fancy or expensive to accomplish that. A $50 car will do just as well as a $50,000 one and save you money as well.

My favorite way to acquire vehicles is by word of mouth; I have had cars given to me that lasted for several years and other vehicles that I have purchased for very little. Ask around to see if anyone has an extra car that they no longer need--chances are you can purchase it for a song and if not move on to the next vehicle.

Ask around at car lots for recent trade-ins that they plan to take to the auction; sometimes they will sell you one of these for very little just to get it off of their inventory.

Visit your local auto auction to purchase your next vehicle in the same method that auto sales places buy them and at wholesale prices as well.

If you don't know much about cars befriend someone who does; they need to go with you to inspect and test-drive the vehicle. Even if you have to hire a mechanic to inspect it you will be ahead of the game. Nothing is more upsetting than buying a car and having it fall apart before you make it to your driveway!

Once you get a vehicle you will need to insure it; older cars can rarely be insured for what they are worth so instead just get basic liability insurance. A few dings won't hurt its drivability and you will save a fortune in insurance costs.

Keep any vehicle you own maintained properly and it will last a long time. If the motor or transmission fails price the replacement of the parts. It may seem too expensive but in the long run you will have a better vehicle than if you purchase a used one off the lot; the motor or transmission will be rebuilt with a warranty instead of just used. So long as the body is in good shape repair that vehicle and continue to use it. If you are conservative with how much you drive you may be able to get 10 or more years out of a cheap used car and all without a single car payment.

Makes you want to laugh all the way to the bank, doesn't it?

FURNITURE, APPLIANCES, ELECTRONICS AND STUFF

Furniture and appliances can take a huge dent out of your budget especially if you finance.

The first thing to consider before acquiring anything is whether or not you really need it; if you don't you have automatically saved money.

If you do, network with family and friends first to see if they know of a free item that you can use.

Next scout thrift shops, yard sales and classifieds to see what you can find. Always bargain for a lower price when appropriate.

Don't settle for something that has fallen apart or broken; there are a ton of gently used pieces of furniture and appliances available. Consumers are taught to upgrade, upgrade, upgrade and rarely wear quality items out before they discard them. These items can be yours for the asking and sometimes YOU will even be asked to help "get rid" of them!

Multi-purpose items are always best when they can be located; the more things an item can do the less individual items you will be forced to buy or find.

Consider how you actually will use an item; traditional pieces may not suit your lifestyle as much as something else. For instance, instead of a couch we have three chairs in our living room. They seat guests comfortably, take up less space, are easier to move around and we always get compliments on how nice our house looks.

Even better: they were free along with the majority of furniture in this house.

Remember that you can always upgrade as time goes along; when you find something better than what you currently own swap the item out and give the old one away if it still has life left in it.

Anything is possible if you know where to look!

TELEVISION

One thing that I did when I moved out on my own was to ditch my television. This was not something that we undertook lightly--in fact it took years to get to the point where we no longer used the device.

First it was a matter of expense: I simply could not afford the $50 monthly cable payment so the kids and I checked out movies from the library, borrowed from friends and rented occasionally to satisfy our television cravings. They grumbled at first but after a while admitted that they really didn't miss it.

When my income went up we splurged on a cable subscription. My kids immediately became glued to that box fighting over the remote. "Mom! Sissy won't let me watch my show!" or "She's got to watch two of her shows--make her give me a turn!"

Having a house guest made it even worse: "Your children are watching XYZ show; are you SURE that is appropriate?" or "Mom, all she wants to do is make us watch game shows all day--we want to watch cartoons!"

I was the one paying the bills yet rarely got to choose a single show on that damned device! Friends told me I needed to buy a couple more televisions to solve the issue.

I just canceled the cable.

Immediately I saw a HUGE change. The kids stopped fighting over the remote, my houseguest moved out and I could actually get close enough to the television to watch a movie of my choice!

There was another benefit I did not expect: my kids no longer barraged me with "can I have this?" When they stopped watching the advertising their requests plummeted. They still saw things that they wanted in the store but apparently the advertising they had seen on television had been a huge driving force behind all of their requests.

I saved a fortune with THAT difference alone.

When we discovered internet streaming our television was used less and less as we migrated to the computer. Sites like 1Channel[11] and Hulu[12] became popular browsing destinations and eventually we realized that our television had sat unused for over a year and so we gave it away.

While we do have laptop computers for both Katie and I we no longer have a television or the expense of a cable bill. Instead we watch our shows and movies online and occasionally check out a movie from the library. Very rarely do we even bother to rent a movie these days because it is too easy to watch for free online, borrow from a friend or locate at the library.

---

[11] http://www.1channel.ch/
[12] http://www.hulu.com/?from=signup

WHAT YOU CAN SAVE

- **Television/televisions**. At several hundred dollars each this is a HUGE savings alone. Older televisions have to have adapters to handle modern digital signals so you almost HAVE to purchase new anymore and if you only have one there are constant fights.

- **Cable bill.** Most cable packages start at around $50 a month. Most of my friends pay a minimum of $100 and up for their cable/satellite packages. They have told me that there are less expensive packages available but these packages don't contain the channels that they actually watch and use.

- **The "I wants**:" the less advertising that your kids are exposed to the less they will beg you to buy. Guaranteed.

HOW TO ELIMINATE YOUR TELEVISION

If your family is addicted to television I recommend a gradual change. Reduce your package as low as you can take it for a few months until the family gets used to having limited options. Encourage them to look online to watch shows if they want more variety. Windows Media Center has a variety of shows, clips and even radio stations that users can watch for free. Make sure that they have access to computers that can play DVDs so that they can watch their movies there instead of on the boob tube. Once they start learning the online sites and how to Google to increase their viewing options cancel the cable/satellite bill entirely.

WATCH MOVIES AND SHOWS FOR FREE ONLINE

There are websites that have movies and television shows available for free streaming. These places are a legal gray area: while it is legal to watch shows on these sites it is frequently not legal to be the one uploading or offering the shows online. As a result these websites come and go; last year the US government shut down a number of them. They come back pretty quickly and a Google search for "watch movies online" will give you a selection to choose from.

Never give out your personal information to these websites and never enter your credit card information. The best sites may offer a premium service but do not take the chance with your money; the legitimate ones will offer a free version supported by advertising.

Here is a list of the sites I currently use and recommend:

http://1channel.ch
http://www.ovguide.com/
http://www.watchfreemovies.ch/

If you want to save the movies that you stream to your computer for offline viewing, download and install the Firefox internet browser and then install the VideoDownloadHelper[13] extension. This way you can discreetly save the videos that you are watching for free so that you can enjoy them even if you are offline.

---

[13] http://www.downloadhelper.net/

VLC[14] is an all-purpose media player that works well with these sites along with JW Player[15]. Install these two programs before you go surfing for movies; some unscrupulous sites will attempt to trick you into installing THEIR versions of this software. If a free website EVER instructs you to download a program to watch their videos leave immediately. Those programs are loaded with spyware and can damage your computer as well as invade your privacy.

COMPUTERS

There is one device that has allowed me to save a fortune. Laptop computers are portable machines that can be used for a variety of things, replacing several traditional devices easily.

The computer I use is an Asus EeePC Touch T101MT. Officially it is classified as a netbook but its small size, reasonable price, excellent battery life and touchscreen have made it my go-to device for daily use.

It runs Windows 7 so I am instantly compatible with the majority of systems out there and when combined with Microsoft Office -- Specifically OneNote -- this machine takes on a life of its own.

---

[14] http://www.videolan.org/vlc/
[15] http://www.longtailvideo.com/players/jw-flv-player/).

My computer replaces a multitude of devices:

- **Home phone.** I use it with a MagicJack, Skype or Google Voice to make phone calls for free anywhere I have Internet access.

- **Cell Phone.** I use my MagicJack, Skype or Google Voice on free Wi-Fi networks and occasionally on cellular broadband to make phone calls for free. It is possible to eliminate cell phones entirely using this method.

- **Stereo.** My entire music collection is on this machine; I carry it everywhere and use it with headphones or without to listen to music. I also use Internet Radio when I desire some listening variety. There are an incredible number of radio stations available on Windows Media Player alone, not including other Internet radio sites such as Shoutcast and Pandora. I flip the screen around to tablet mode so that I can just tap the screen when I want to change songs without having to deal with a mouse or touchpad. I have included a list of free internet radio sites in the References section.

- **Library.** All of the books I purchase these days are digital and I have eliminated all but a few physical books that I have yet to locate digital replacements for. I can keep my book library with me for whenever I have a few minutes to read or I need to reference something in one of my books. This one machine is lighter than a number of the books I use and digital copies are less expensive than their physical counterparts. This also gives me immense satisfaction because I am not contributing to the death of trees to satisfy my literary cravings.

- **Television.** Instead of a traditional television I use my computer. I can connect an external DVD or Blu-Ray drive to the system to watch movies wherever I desire. I also keep digital copies of my favorite movies on my computer and watch a lot of movies online. See the section titled "Ditch Your Television" for more information.

- **Portable DVD player.** My laptop has a 6.5 hour battery life and with an inverter I can connect it to my van and use it even longer. Katie loves watching movies on long trips but instead of splurging on a separate DVD player we just use our laptops.

- **Day Planner.** This computer is small enough to take with me so I use Microsoft Office to keep track of any appointments or important dates. Since I only use one device for this I have nothing to sync. Microsoft Hotmail has an online calendar and address book that you can view in Outlook if you do need to sync these items across multiple computers.

- **Notepad.** This computer has the ability to recognize handwriting when used with Windows 7 Home Premium and higher. I flip the screen around and hand write grocery lists, letters and any other items that I would use a notepad for.

- **Journal.** I can hand write or type out my journal entries as desired. I use OneNote so that I can sync them all to the cloud and not concern myself with backups. Anyone who comes after me will be able to access all of my notes, both in my handwriting and typed in a single location.

- **Sketchpad.** I use Microsoft Paint to draw in tablet mode instead of purchasing and keeping up with artist's materials. If I desire a hard copy I can print it out on regular or photograph paper in whatever size I desire.

- **File Cabinet.** I scan all of my important documents and save them to my computer as well as sync them to the cloud. This way my important documents are all in one place and a simple search is all it takes to locate whatever document I need.

- **Alarm Clock.** I use a free alarm clock program[16] to wake up in the mornings instead of investing in a separate device. Since my computer is always with me I see no logic in having clocks scattered all over creation or buying a watch to wear.

- **Communication Device.** I use Yahoo Messenger, Skype or Google Voice to send and receive text messages on my computer. I also use my computer to access email and social networking sites to keep track of friends and family instead of picking up the phone. It is easier, convenient, faster and less expensive than traditional methods of communication.

- **Fax machine.** I use Faxzero.com to send short faxes for free but if I wanted to connect a modem to this computer Windows 7 has the ability to send and receive faxes through a traditional phone line. I have even used a modem to send and receive faxes through my MagicJack in the past; currently I insist that people send me documents through email because it is much more convenient.

- **Camera.** I have an external webcam aside from the webcam that is built into this computer; by placing the computer in tablet mode and facing the webcam forward I have a high-quality camera for no extra cost. Why buy a camera when you have something that works just as well already?

A little-known fact about computers is that you can continue to use older computers even if their operating system is out of date. Ubuntu Linux is an operating system that requires less resources than modern versions of Microsoft Windows and is completely free. It has a huge repository of programs available for free with a

---

[16] Alarm Clock Program (free download):
http://download.cnet.com/Free-Alarm-Clock/3000-2350_4-75328290.html?tag=rb_content;contentBody

couple of clicks and is so easy to use even little kids can figure it out. It is also very stable and is not afflicted with the viruses that are so common in Windows machines. I have included a list of links to a variety of free operating systems in the References section.

If you have a REALLY old computer you can breathe life back into it using DSL Linux[17] (a.k.a. Damn Small Linux). I kept an old Windows 95 laptop alive and useful for many years past its prime using this operating system. I could surf the internet, check my email, play games, listen to music, write in my journal and do many other things with that machine until the hardware finally gave out. It is an excellent way to get the full use out of those old computers you have stuffed in the back of your closet!

WHAT ABOUT A MAC?

Apple computers are wonderful, beautiful machines. I have seen these machines outlast the functionality of similar Windows machines by several years. Walk into the computer lab of a public school and you will discover iMacs that came out in the days of Windows 98 still going strong and in active use by the students there. They are truly the Energizer bunnies of the computer industry!

---

[17] http://damnsmalllinux.org/

If you are not very skilled with computers get a Mac. They are easy to learn, use and have excellent tech support from Apple. They cost more but you get what you pay for.

Confession: I do not own an Apple device though I have in the past. I prefer a single device to act as both a tablet and a laptop computer and Apple does not have an offering currently that addresses that need. I have worked on Apple machines for friends and clients in the past; I find them to be excellent machines and worthy of the accolades that they receive.

WINDOWS SOFTWARE ON A SHOESTRING

If you are using Microsoft Windows you have an inexpensive software option that is legal and will save you a fortune. Go to Waysale.com[18] and check out their software section. This is the website I use to keep up to date versions of Windows and Office as well as acquire any other software I need. It is legal and legitimate.

The reason these prices are so cheap is that businesses sell to other countries for far less than they sell to those of us in the US. They acquire the rights to resell the software and we benefit from the sizeable discount they receive for being in another country. In fact, you will download any Microsoft software directly from Microsoft itself so have no fears; I use them myself.

---

[18] http://www.waysale.com/softwares

TORRENTS

Torrents are a method of file sharing that can be used to download movies, music, books and other items. It is a peer-to-peer network; you may download pieces of a single file from hundreds of individual computers. Some of the more popular sites are ISOHunt[19] and The Pirate Bay[20]. You need a program called a torrent client to use these sites: one of the more popular ones is called uTorrent[21].

Torrents have pretty much replaced the older Napster-like clients that proliferated in the wilder days of the Internet; agencies like the RIAA and the MPAA know this. As a result they watch these torrents and will notify your ISP if they catch your internet address downloading illegal files. Since a good portion of the files on these sites are illegal it is best to avoid them *especially* if you are using a personal internet connection.

Note: Bad things can happen if you get caught sharing files illegally. Here are a couple of links for you to see yourself:

http://www.cbsnews.com/stories/2007/10/04/national/main333018
6.shtml
http://www.msnbc.msn.com/id/32236444/ns/technology_and_scie
nce-security

---

[19] http://www.isohunt.com
[20] http://thepiratebay.se
[21] http://www.utorrent.com/

Be safe and avoid these sites unless you are downloading legal content like open source software. While it is not necessarily illegal to view streamed music and video it is definitely illegal to be caught uploading and sharing it. Torrent and file sharing sites will not only allow you to download but automatically share those files as well. Avoid them.

After a while when using these methods your family will rely more and more upon viewing shows on the computer instead of on the television; you can then eliminate the televisions one by one until there is a single unused machine and then ditch that too.

Laugh as your neighbors go broke while they continue to feed the machine.

BOOKS, MUSIC AND OTHER STUFF

I am a bibliophile. While I may no longer own a wall lined with books I read more now than ever.

Anyone who desires to live a free, frugal life should do the same. Knowledge is power and it has never been easier to gain the knowledge that we need to grow.

It doesn't take a fortune either.

I make less in a month that a good portion of the United States brings home in a week. Even with that I am able to read about any subject I desire and listen to what I enjoy as well.

THE LIBRARY

The library is a wonderful source for information. Most libraries now carry books, music and movies. Some even allow online access to digital materials. If you live in a small town your selection will doubtless be limited and if you don't have a way to get there you are screwed entirely. That's okay because there are other ways to feed your mind.

THE INTERNET

You can find an incredible number of free books online. Online ebook retailers have a number of books offered for free. Project Gutenberg is one source for free ebooks that I have used for years. There are different books available at the Australian website. If you are looking for a particular older book check out both of these sites.

Google Books also has a large archive available to search as well as the Internet Archive. If you are researching a spiritual subject you may want to check out the Sacred Texts Archive. They have an incredible amount of books available for viewing online. They are an excellent resource for the original New Thought books from writers like Wallace Wattles, Robert Collier, Florence Scovel Shinn and others. Free Ebooks.net is another site I have recently discovered that is loaded with free ebooks along with ManyBooks.net. You could read for years without paying a single penny! I have included all of these links in the References section.

GOOGLE

Google is one of my favorite ways to find free books. You can use any search engine really; I typically try more than one on a good search. It's like going on a treasure hunt.

Type in the title of the book, music or movie that you are looking for and the format desired.

Like this:
Book Title PDF
Or
Movie Title AVI
Or
Song Title MP3

Try different formats if you can't get any hits on the first one. Books commonly come in PDF, Mobi, RTF and TXT formats. Movies come in AVI, FLV and MOV most commonly and songs typically are ripped in MP3, OGG, WAV, FLAC and WMA.

The three most common formats are PDF, AVI and MP3 because they are usually not copy protected or DRMed

If it is legal in your area add the word "torrent" (without the quotes) to the search string. This allows you to search for torrents that are floating around.

It takes time and patience to find stuff like this. It is *much* quicker to buy a digital copy if it is available.

WARNING: While this is technically possible, some consider this method neither moral nor ethical. Sometimes it is the only way to locate an older out of print book that your dog chewed up or a really old song after your record player dies. Let your conscience guide you. I am not your mother so I'm not going to slap your fingers if I catch you typing this on a keyboard. That said, your own mother might hit more than your fingers if she catches you mining the Internet using these tricks. Or worse you could land in court if this is illegal in your area so check your laws and cover your butt.

GENERAL SUBJECTS

If you are interested in a particular subject scour the search engines. There are a huge number of websites out there and many of them will contain information pertinent to whatever it is you want to know. For instance, if you suddenly find yourself having to live in your car, type that in and you will find a huge resource of information to help you cope with your situation.

That's what I did when I started camping in my van and I still use some of that knowledge today. That's also what I did when I first moved out with my kids to learn how to live on less--but that's another story.

The Internet is the new encyclopedia and you don't have to be rich to afford a copy. Just schlep on over to some place with free Wi-Fi and drink the information down.

THRIFT SHOPS, YARD SALES AND OTHER RESOURCES

Thrift shops are at once a wonderful thing and a horrible temptation. Not only can you locate things that you need and will use at incredible prices but you also have to wade through a bunch of useless (and sometimes overpriced) junk.

I try to go to thrift shops occasionally with a specific goal (a new shirt, for example) in mind. I have gotten to the point now where I can safely browse without the desire to take everything home but until I reached that point I spent more than I actually used.

For instance, you go into a thrift shop in search of the perfect sweater. You find not just that sweater but 4 more. You buy them all, take them home and within a few days realize that you have worn the first one or two you purchased but have no desire to wear the other two. Those two ended up being a waste of your time and money.

Kids and thrift shops can be fun. Give them a limit and let them explore. It is cheaper than the Dollar Store, much better quality and you will have a huge amount of your wallet left when they are finished.

Katie feels like a queen when we go thrifting and always brings home a stuffed animal or two.

I look at the thrift shops for any purchase that I'm considering. That was how I bought my latest toaster oven for $4--a device that gets used almost daily around here. We also bought Katie's school uniforms there and paid less than half of what we would have paid in a retail store.

THRIFT SHOP RULES

- **Inspect each item thoroughly**. If it is broken or otherwise damaged do not purchase. Some cosmetic blemishes are acceptable but don't buy with the intention to "fix" it. It won't get fixed if you take it home unless you repair it as soon as you carry it through the door.
- **Check the size carefully**. Try on any clothing items because some sizes may be different from what you expect them to be.
- Always plug in electronic items to **verify that they work before you purchase**. Some shops do not have return policies.
- **If you are unsure** about compatibility with something you already own **do not purchase**. The odds are that it won't match and you will have wasted your money. If you are looking for something in particular bring the item to be matched with you or enough information to guarantee compatibility.
- **Avoid old software**. The chances of it requiring an installation code are high and if you don't have the code for that disc it is useless. Some software (particularly Microsoft software) requires activation and will only allow activation a certain number of times or on certain hardware configurations. Go online and download something for free instead.
- **Only buy what you can actually use**. Don't stock up unless it is an item you are positive you will use before it goes bad. For instance I once owned a cordless phone that took a specific battery. I found a pile of them in the clearance aisle for a buck each. I bought all

of them and before I went through the first two the phone died and I was unable to locate a compatible model.

Regardless of the caveats thrift shops are wonderful places. Those are my favorite shops to visit and most of our wardrobes come from there.

YARD SALES

Yard sales are great if you have the time, energy and desire to run all over the countryside looking for them (and through them).

I love yard sales but I don't go out in search of them. If I happen to stumble upon one when I have the time we enjoy looking and we have found some incredible deals. For instance, Katie found a huge box of beanie baby cards at one sale that we purchased for $5. They have amused her for hours as she trades with her friends so I consider that a good investment. Another thing I picked up at a recent sale was a set of those reusable lint rollers that you clean by running under a stream of water. The price was fifty cents--well less than a $3 disposable lint roller at the store. It works well and has easily lasted long enough to justify the cost.

Always deal in cash when you shop at yard sales **and be prepared to barter**. If you see something in particular that you would like to purchase it sometimes helps to place the amount of the offer in a particular pocket (out of view of the yard sale host, of course) and then tell the person that you are interested in a certain item but all you have is a certain amount of cash. A lot of times if your offer is reasonable they will accept the offer. Just be careful not to let them see that you have more money than you offered or it could spoil the fun for other bargain hunters. This was how we got the Beanie Baby cards so cheap. They were actually priced for $15 but I told the lady all I had on me to spare was $5 after I made some other purchases. She accepted without a pause.

When you make a good bargain load up your purchases quickly and leave. You don't want the host to have second thoughts or to overhear you bragging about your good fortune.

If you enjoy driving around and shopping take a day and go yard sailing. It is fun, frugal and you can locate some wonderful finds. Don't forget to bargain--you get the best deals that way.

AUCTIONS

Auctions can be a source of incredible deals but you can easily overspend if you bid in the heat of the moment. Estate and storage building auctions can be a wonderful source of frugal purchases. Arrive early enough to look around and decide which particular items you are interested in bidding on.

When you choose what to bid upon make a mental list of how high you are willing to bid. If you are bidding on several items you may want to make a physical list with the prices you are willing to pay. No matter how excited you get or how fast and passionate the bidding gets DO NOT go over your agreed high bid.

CRAIGSLIST, FREECYCLE AND OTHER ONLINE RESOURCES

Craigslist (http://www.craigslist.org) and Freecycle (http://www.freecycle.org) are wonderful online ways to acquire and eliminate stuff. I have used them numerous times and find them to be excellent resources.

Should you decide to try them please be safe. Only agree to meet people in a public place and never put your address or personal information out in the public posts.

There are a number of area-specific classified ad websites throughout the world; ask your friends, neighbors and visit your town's official websites to determine the links for your area. You can also Google for "(town name) classifieds" or search Topix (http://www.topix.net) for the links as well.

Warning: Topix is a hotbed of viciousness and rumors. Just search it for what you need and leave. To get sucked into that website is NOT fun.

GROCERIES, RECIPES AND GROW YOUR OWN

L ife on a shoestring does not mean eating beans and rice every day; we eat a variety of foods and never go hungry or without something we crave. The main difference between our diet and the average American diet is that we don't eat out very often and we rarely purchase convenience foods.

STAPLES

I keep our pantry stocked with a variety of staples; we mix and match these with items we find on sale or we happen to be craving.

- Ramen noodles (both cup Ramen and the packaged Ramen). We use these in other meals and for when we want a quick dinner.
- Clearance meat (we always watch for specials and stock up when we find them)
- Canned and/or frozen vegetables. I grew up mostly on canned vegetables and still keep a supply on hand. These are purchased on sale in larger quantities throughout the year. We generally serve at least one vegetable at every meal but we prefer 2 vegetables per meal.
- Fresh fruits and vegetables when in-season and on sale. We grow a few vegetables like bell peppers, tomatoes, snow peas and squash but we also glean from neighbor's gardens when we have permission.
- Dried beans. We rotate which beans we use depending upon our mood. Some of the beans we eat are:
  - Navy beans

- Pinto beans
- Black beans
- Lima beans
- Lentils (cooked and sprouted)
- 15 bean soup (occasional treat because of price)
- Kidney beans
- Great Northern beans
- Soybeans (used to make soymilk)
- Mung beans (sprouted)
- Bread. Sometimes I bake it from scratch using whole wheat (or grinding wheat berries in the blender). Homemade bread is more filling than store-bought.
- Rice.
- Powdered milk. I keep this on hand if I don't have a supply of soybeans to make milk with when we run out (or are low on money).
- Egg noodles.
- Potatoes.
- Fresh onions.
- Oatmeal. This is used for breakfast, dessert and an addition to some meals.
- Peanut butter.
- Jelly.

MILK

If you can't use a whole gallon of milk at a time place half of it in the refrigerator and freeze the other half until you are ready for it. Just thaw in the refrigerator, shake well and serve. The freezer "pauses" the expiration date on the container so count out how many days were left on the container when you froze it to calculate the new expiration date. For instance, a container of milk had a week left before it expired. You froze it for a month and then placed it in the refrigerator to thaw. Your new expiration date would be one week after you took it out of the freezer.

Powdered milk used to be a big money saver but the stores have caught on to us Frugalistas and have raised the price. It is still good to keep on hand for those times when you run out of milk and don't want to drop everything for a trip to the grocery store.

A pound of soybeans makes a gallon of soymilk; purchased in bulk you can have this healthy substitute for cow's milk at a price considerably lower than you can purchase cow's milk in the store.

SHOPPING AND MEAL PLANNING

I generally don't shop with a set plan; I make sure to keep staples on hand and then stock up on sale items like meats. If I know that the price of something (like peanut butter and coffee) is going up I make sure to buy several to hopefully ride out the price storm.

Meals are planned maybe a day in advance. We look around the house and work on leftovers first (since we're picky about leftovers we actually try to avoid them) then we create a meal with things we have on hand. Our average everyday meal is a small piece of meat and one or two vegetables. Breakfast is oatmeal, cereal, yogurt with granola or cream of wheat. Occasionally we splurge on a country breakfast (eggs, bacon/ham, biscuits, jelly and grits) but I have to be in a cooking mood to do that much work!

Baked potatoes are a standby for those days when we really don't feel like cooking. They also get served up a lot for lunch because we love them. We toss everything on them from cheese, ranch dressing, bacon bits, black olives, sour cream and anything else we have laying around that looks good.

RECIPES

We have a few tried-and-true recipes that we love. Some of these were passed down from my parents and grandparents and others have been picked up here and there. I've even got a few that I came up with personally.

NURSE AIDE CHILI

The name of this chili originated because I learned this recipe in a nurse's aide class many years ago. I didn't enjoy the class but I really loved their chili!

- 1 pound ground beef
- 1 pound dried kidney beans
- Large can or jar of V8 juice (substitute tomato juice if needed)
- Chili powder to taste (we use approx. 1/4 of a small chili powder jar)
- Onions (optional)
- 2 cups water

Soak the kidney beans overnight and then drain the water. Add the water and can of V8 juice to the beans and start cooking the next day. Add water as needed and cook until the beans are tender.

Brown the ground beef and pour off the fat. Add to the bean/v8 mixture along with the chili powder and onions. Cook for approx. 15 minutes.

If you have a ripe tomato in your garden chop it up and add it to the mix.

Quick Cook Method: Substitute 2-3 cans of kidney beans for the dried beans. Add browned ground beef, onions, chili powder and V8 and then cook for 15-20 minutes.

We eat this chili with shredded cheese and peanut butter sandwiches one day, on hot dogs the next, as a chili sandwich the third day then make a "taco salad" with the last bits (pour the chili over nacho chips). This is one meal that has zero waste in our household.

RAMEN SUPREME

- 2 packages of Ramen noodles (Beef or chicken depending upon the meat we use)
- Water
- 1 pound of ground beef, chicken or turkey, browned or drained. You can also use Little Smokies, sliced Polish sausage, sliced hot dogs or any other type of meat you have hanging around. Just cut the meat into small pieces and cook thoroughly before adding it to the recipe.

Boil the water. Crumble the Ramen noodles and add to the water. Cook until the noodles are done and then drain. Add the seasoning packet and the meat. Cook until thoroughly heated through and mixed.

Variations: You can substitute a couple of scrambled eggs instead of the meat, add a dash of soy sauce or add some vegetables to this. The possibilities are endless which make it the perfect standby meal.

MOM'S MAC AND CHEESE

This recipe was discovered one night when I realized we were out of milk while cooking. I grabbed the first thing I could think of (extra butter and mayo) and discovered a new favorite meal.

- Box of cheap mac and cheese.
- Milk (check the side of the package to verify the amount). If you are out of milk, increase the butter and mayo. The kids won't even notice.
- Butter (check the package for amount).
- Heaping tablespoon of real mayonnaise. (don't use light mayonnaise or Miracle Whip; it has to be real full-fat mayo).
- Handful of grated cheese. This can be American, Velveeta, Cheddar, Parmesan, Mozzarella--whatever cheese you happen to have on hand.

Prepare the mac and cheese according to the package directions but add the mayonnaise along with the flavoring packet. Sprinkle the cheese on top (or mix it in) right before you serve it.

Variations: To make cheeseburger macaroni, brown 1/2 pound (or a whole pound if you have it) and add to the mac and cheese. Heat until thoroughly mixed.

POOR MAN'S MEAL

- 1-2 eggs, beaten
- 1-2 diced potatoes
- 1/2 onion, diced
- Salt
- Pepper
- Tablespoon of Salsa
- Oil for cooking

- Crumbled bacon, sliced hot dog, sliced Polish sausage, crumbled breakfast sausage or small pieces of any meat you may have available (optional)

Place a splash of oil in a skillet and heat until warm. Add the meat, diced potatoes and onion. Season with salt and pepper, cover and then cook until the potatoes are tender. Add water if desired to keep from sticking and increase softness of the potatoes.

Add the beaten eggs and stir into the potato mixture. Cook until the eggs are done. Stir in the salsa and serve.

Variation: Sprinkle shredded cheese on top before serving if desired.

This meal can be served as breakfast or dinner.

TUNAPEA SALAD
- 1 can tuna
- 2 tablespoons cold leftover peas
- 1-2 tablespoons mayonnaise

Open and drain the can of tuna and dump into a bowl. Add the peas (more or less according to taste). Mix in the mayonnaise to taste and serve on crackers or bread.

BASIC ROAST
This is the roast we cook most often. We prefer boneless chuck roasts with the grain of the meat running vertically instead of horizontally because those pieces seem to be more tender.

- 1 boneless chuck roast
- 1 packet of French Onion Soup Mix
- 4-5 large carrots, cut into chunks

- 2-3 large potatoes, washed and cut into chunks
- 1/2 of an onion, diced
- Water

Place the roast in the center of the baking pan. Use a baking pan with high sides to accommodate the vegetables.

Place the vegetables around the roast. Sprinkle the French Onion Soup Mix over both meat and vegetables. Pour 1/2 inch of water into the pan. Cover and place in a 350°F oven. Check and baste every hour. The meat will flake with a fork when done. Remove the cover during the last 15 minutes of cooking to brown the meat and vegetables. Serve immediately.

Variations: Instead of French Onion soup mix substitute Cream of Mushroom soup. Other options are adding a packet of brown gravy mix along with (or instead of) the soup mix and using seasoning salt instead of soup mix.

BREAKFAST RECIPES

FRENCH TOAST

- A couple of eggs. (Use more or less depending upon how many slices of toast you plan to make). I generally start with 2-3 eggs and add more as the mix gets low in the bowl.
- Cinnamon powder.
- Teaspoon of vanilla. We normally just pour a good splash into the bowl without measuring.
- 2 Tablespoons of milk. We have also used cream, half and half and evaporated milk. It tastes delicious either way. If you are short on eggs use more milk to stretch it.

- Bread. This can be old bread, fresh bread, homemade bread or whatever you have on hand. Just don't use garlic or other similarly seasoned breads (cinnamon bread would be good though) because it will detract from the end result. You can use 1-2 pieces of bread per egg.
- Butter or oil for frying.

Crack the eggs into a shallow bowl. Use a fork or whisk to scramble them thoroughly. Add a few sprinkles of cinnamon, vanilla and milk. Mix well.

Place a dollop of butter or oil in the skillet and heat. You can tell the skillet is ready if a drop of water sizzles and immediately evaporates.

Place a slice of bread into the egg mixture, allow it to soak for a moment and then flip to coat both sides well. The longer you leave it in the mix the more egg will soak up, the longer you will need to cook it and the less pieces of toast you will be able to make per batch.

Place the coated bread into the heated skillet. Cook until one side is done and then flip to cook the other side. Serve warm with syrup.

SYRUP IN A PINCH

If you run out of syrup use this recipe. We take spells where we prefer it to store-bought. It is definitely much less expensive than store bought even when you add fruit to it.

- 2 cups sugar
- 1 cup water
- 1 Tablespoon vanilla or Maple extract

Pour the sugar and water into a pan and heat on the stove, stirring constantly. Allow to boil for 5 minutes or until the mixture resembles a thin syrup. Add the vanilla or maple extract and stir to mix. Serve immediately over French toast or pancakes.

Note: You can also add fruit like blueberries, apples or others to this syrup to make a fruity syrup.

BEVERAGES

THE WATER BOTTLE

One necessity for living on a shoestring is a water bottle. This should be made of stainless steel instead of plastic or aluminum; both plastic and aluminum will leach unwanted chemicals into your water.

This bottle is kept filled and with you at all times so that you always have a drink available when you are thirsty. At no point should anything other than water be placed in this bottle for both sanitary and health reasons but it is acceptable to add a splash of lemon for flavor.

Water is the original drink and is much healthier than the soft drinks and juices on the market today. Use a pitcher water filter to have clean water for pennies or allow tap water to sit uncovered for a few minutes to eliminate unwanted chlorine and other gasses from tap water.

This saves you money, eliminating the temptation to purchase unhealthy and expensive soft drinks. Drink at least 1/2 ounce of water per pound of body weight and occasionally place a few grains of salt on your tongue for optimum benefit. Read <u>Water: For Health, for healing, for Life: You're Not Sick, You're Thirsty!</u> by Dr. F. Batmanghelidj for more information. You can also visit Watercure.com to explore more books by the same author.

When you use your water bottle all of the time it will eventually need to be cleaned; you can delay this by rinsing it well with hot water once a day.

Clean your water bottle by filling it half full of hot water and add a teaspoon of washing soda, borax or baking soda. Cap the bottle and shake well before pouring out and rinsing with more hot water. Allow to air dry completely. This does well to keep any unpleasant odors at bay but without the soap that can coat the inside and affect the taste.

SOYMILK

This soymilk is all-natural and contains no preservatives. I like to keep a supply of soybeans on hand and make this up as I need it so we always have a fresh batch available.

- 4 ounces (1/4 pound) raw soybeans

- 1 quart water
- 1 teaspoon vanilla (optional)
- 1 teaspoon sugar (optional)

Soak soybeans in water overnight. If you are in a hurry bring them to a boil on the stove for ten minutes instead. This will change the flavor of the soymilk however.

Drain the soybeans and place in a blender. Add 1 quart of water. Blend until liquefied. Strain through a cheesecloth to remove the okara (fibrous part of the soybean). You can squeeze the okara to make sure you get all of the soymilk out.

Heat the soymilk to a boil for 3 minutes, stirring constantly. Add the vanilla and sugar then mix well. Allow to cool and refrigerate.

Makes 1 quart of soymilk.

GROW YOUR OWN FOOD

Gardens are wonderful things. You can have food that is healthy and safe, raised to your personal standards and it doesn't have to cost a fortune. You don't even need a lot of equipment.

The first rule to gardening is to **only grow what you will actually eat**. If you don't eat tomatoes, don't plant a whole row of them. Perhaps have a plant or two for salads and soups (or for fried green tomatoes) but don't plant an ungodly ton of them. I have seen huge sections of gardens with tomatoes rotting on the vine simply because of overplanting.

The second rule to gardening is to **avoid planting items that you can find in a grocery store cheaper** than you can raise them. An excellent example of this is carrots. These come on sale frequently and rarely cost very much so buy them in a store instead of raising them.

The third rule is to **raise your garden in as small of a space as possible** so that you can minimize the amount of area that you have to dig, plant, weed, fertilize and care for. Square Foot and kiddie pool gardens are excellent options, especially if you have poor soil. I have included links to both of these methods in the References section of this book.

The fourth rule is to **get creative** and think outside of the gardening box. If you enjoy raising sunflowers or corn plant some beans or peas near your plants and train them to grow up the tall plants. This provides a natural trellis for free, using space that you would normally be using anyway. Sow squash and pumpkin seeds beneath your taller plants to provide a natural ground cover and reduce the amount of weeding that you have to do as well as maximize the amount of vegetables you can grow in the same space. Using this method means you can harvest 3, 4 or even more crops in the space you would normally plant just one.

PLANT A THREE SISTERS GARDEN

Native Americans were firm believers in companion planting. They would make a mound of dirt and dig several small holes in the hill.

Within these holes they would place pieces of fish they acquired for this purpose and add some corn seeds. When the corn would sprout they would then plant beans, and after the beans sprouted they would add squash or pumpkin seeds. The fish would rot and fertilize the plants, the corn provided a natural trellis for the beans, the beans create nitrogen to additionally fertilize the corn and squash, while the squash provide ground cover to prevent weeds around the corn and beans. Each item worked together to provide for each other.

GROW POTATOES WITHOUT DIGGING

If you have a piece of wire fencing you can make an above ground potato bin and toss in your potato peels to have potatoes for virtually free:

Loop the wire fencing around to make a tunnel and stand it upon its end. It should look like a wire barrel. Place this in a sunny spot in your garden or in your front yard.

Toss some straw or yard clippings into the bottom of the wire bin. Make sure there is an inch or two in there. Take some potatoes that have sprouted (those potatoes in your pantry you forgot about are perfect) and cut them into sections with a clean knife. Make sure there is an eye or sprout on each potato piece and that each piece is at least a couple of inches in size. If in doubt don't cut them at all just dump them in whole. Position the potato pieces so that they are not touching each other. If they touch they will probably rot instead of sprout.

Cover this with some more straw, hay or yard waste. If you can get some free mulch grab it and add to the mix. Place an inch or so on top of the potato pieces.

As the potato plants grow add more mulch, straw, hay and yard clippings to the bin. You can also add other plant waste like vegetable scraps to the bin. Cover the plants but allow about an inch or so of the plant to show at all times.

The potatoes will keep growing and will also grow out of the sides of the wire bin as well. Keep adding yard waste and straw to the bin until you reach the top of the wire. Water well and wait until the plants die naturally and then open the bin at the side. The potatoes will fall out and you will have an amazing harvest!

You can also grow potatoes in large trash cans. I have included a link in the references about the method.

Another way to plant your potato bin is to use just the peels from the potatoes. As you use potatoes in your regular cooking be generous when you are peeling and take off more of the potato than you normally would. Toss these into your bin and lightly cover. Some of these will sprout and then you just keep the plants covered with the mulch.

When I was a kid we never threw away potato peels. Dad kept a trench dug and we would scatter our peelings in a section of the trench to cover and forget about. In the fall I was always amazed at how many "volunteer" potatoes we harvested as a result!

FOOD STORAGE METHODS

Once you grow your food you will want to store it for the winter. Some items like beans, corn and peas can be allowed to dry on the plant before being harvested and stored. Rehydrate these as needed for cooking.

Other foods can be canned, frozen or dehydrated. I personally do not can because canning foods can become terribly expensive when you factor in the cost of the jars, pressure cooker, water canner and other supplies. However if you can acquire the jars for cheap or free this is an economical way to store food. Be warned that it is very labor-intensive.

Most foods can be easily frozen for later use. If you are careful to bag or otherwise protect your foods prior to freezing they will last a bit longer than recommended freezer storage methods claim.

FREEZING FRESH CORN

If you want to freeze fresh corn do not shuck it. The shuck will provide a layer of protection and keep it fresh for much longer in the freezer. Harvest your corn by pulling it from the stalk and then bag it in a heavy freezer bag unshucked.

DEHYDRATION

Dehydrators can be used to preserve a variety of foods easily and safely. You can store the dried foods in the pantry or in a freezer. In my experience dehydrated foods keep longer in the freezer because they are not exposed to excess moisture in there but it is not a requirement.

RAISING ANIMALS FOR MEAT

I spent a number of my childhood years watching animals be raised and slaughtered for food. We worked hard to provide the creatures with a good life and a quick death - as painless as we were able to provide. Our logic was that we provided as much of a loving environment for the animals as possible in gratitude for the gift of life they were to give us.

Today's modern homes may not have room for the more common meats served at the dinner table. Cows and pigs can take up a lot of space! You can keep a pig in a smaller area like in a wooden bin raised off of the ground to prevent them from rooting.

PIGS

I have seen pigs grown in those raised and covered bins and they don't seem to be happy - they have a natural love of the earth and while they may grow fat in these places I don't believe I could personally raise one that way. It is a simple matter to just let them live in a lot on the dirt. They get to be close to the earth that they love which seems much more humane.

While you can feed hogs with scraps, slop and enriched pig feed for the majority of their life, in order to achieve the best tasting meat only feed them cracked corn for the last 2-3 weeks before slaughter. My father said this cleaned out their systems; I know there is a difference in how the meat tastes in pork that is only fed corn in those last few weeks and I personally prefer it.

Cows

A cow raised for meat does not need a huge area to roam if you keep an ample supply of cracked corn available for them to eat. Cows don't chew very thoroughly so whole corn is passed through their system undigested; make sure to give them cracked corn so that they can get the full use of the nutrients.

To slaughter a cow you will need something strong and tall to lift him up to bleed and prepare him on; we used a tripod that the neighbors pulled car engines with. Cows, like all animals, have reflexes that activate while they are dying and shortly after death this causes them to kick out. This can be VERY dangerous if you are kicked by a cow. It is MUCH safer to haul your cow to a slaughterhouse known for killing animals humanely than it is to kill and dress him at home.

Milk cows are a lot of work; you have to breed them once a year and then either sell the calf or keep him separated from his mother for a good part of the day in order to acquire a portion of the milk he would normally drink. Once she gives birth to the calf you allow the calf full reign of his mother's teats for the first week and then separate the pair. You will then milk the cow at least twice a day (every 12 hours) after which you allow the calf to nurse with his mother. The more frequently you milk her the more often the calf gets to feed which is easier on the calf. For best results milk two of the teats, allow the calf to nurse and then strip out the milk from all of the teats. Some save this milk to bottle feed the calf while others feed it to cats and other animals.

I personally feel bad stealing a baby calf's milk and depriving him of his mother's love and companionship. That is one of the reasons I prefer soymilk but I will purchase whole milk from a farmer who treats his calves humanely.

Once you acquire the milk from the cow allow it to sit in the bucket or other wide-mouth container (a bowl is excellent for this) for at least 24 hours until the cream rises to the top. Scoop off the cream with a cup or a deep spoon; this cream can be used as-is for cooking or churned to make butter.

You don't need a churn for butter but it does make it a LOT easier. As a child my father churned butter by hand in a wide-mouth jar. He would pour the cream into the jar and then we would take turns shaking it. The constant agitation would make the butter. We would strain out the butter using cheesecloth and then pack it into plastic containers for freezing. You can add some salt to the butter before storage if desired. There is nothing in this world that tastes like home-churned butter! Once you have it you will never look at store-bought butter or margarine the same.

Note: Do not add salt to the cream *before* you churn it. This will prevent the butter from forming. The liquid left over from churning the butter is real honest-to-goodness buttermilk for you to enjoy. Like the butter you make it will taste nothing like the store-bought stuff.

GOATS

Goats are smaller than cows and can be kept in much smaller spaces. They love to eat and have even been used as living lawn mowers[22] for some major tech companies. They produce milk that some find easier to digest then cow's milk and can also be used as meat.

CHICKENS

Chickens are a great animal for smaller spaces. They provide meat, eggs and feathers in exchange for their keep. A small shed with roosting boxes allows them to be sheltered at night; during the day you can allow them to run in your yard to keep insects under control. You won't have to worry about fleas, roaches, beetles or other insects if you have a flock of chickens running loose but be warned - they poop a lot and it gets everywhere!

---

[22] http://www.foxnews.com/story/0,2933,518820,00.html

Don't let them run free in areas where children play or you want to maintain cleanliness because they leave copious droppings.

When I was a kid it was a daily chore to help my grandparents harvest eggs. A single egg would be given a mark with a pencil and placed in each nesting box; this would encourage the chickens to lay in the boxes instead of looking for other places to hide their eggs. You would reach under the chickens and remove the eggs that did not contain this mark. *Be warned*: some hens like to peck at you when you do this!

When you want to hatch a brood of chicks allow one hen to rest undisturbed. Do not take her eggs; just leave her be to do her thing. In a few weeks she will hatch out a batch of chicks and care for them lovingly. Mother hens are very protective; some will flog anyone or anything that gets close to her young brood while others will let their handlers look at the chicks.

Most people would purchase a large amount of pullets from the local feed store in the spring instead of allowing their hens to set on the eggs. This provided a large number of chickens the same age so that all of them could be slaughtered at the same time. These animals would be allowed to grow until slaughtering day.

On slaughtering day an area would be set up with knives, freezer bags and containers for the offal. A big metal barrel with an opening cut in the side would be placed upon a fire and filled with water. Once the water boiled the killing would begin.

The chickens were caught by the children and given to the adults who would wring their necks with a jerk. Sometimes the heads would pop off and the animals would flop around on the ground in reaction. This was upsetting to us kids at first but we were shown that the animal was dead the moment his head left his body; it was a muscle reaction as the final electrical impulses were expended.

After the chickens were killed they were handed back to the kids who held them by the legs and dipped them into the boiling water. We swished them around for a few minutes and then removed them. We would then grab their feathers and attempt to pull them off. The removed feathers were saved in bags for use in feather pillows and mattresses. If the feathers didn't come off we dipped them in the hot water again and again until we were able to remove all of the feathers. They were then passed back to the adults who gutted them, rinsed them well and packed them whole into freezer bags for later use. One or two chickens would be kept out for a feast to celebrate the end of slaughtering day and the children were rewarded with treats and praised for their good work. I have included a link in the Resources section about making feather pillows and mattresses.

RABBITS

Local ordinances have made it harder for the practitioner of the shoestring lifestyle to grow meat at home. If you live in urban areas you will probably be prohibited from raising traditional animals like cows, pigs, goats and chickens.

Rabbits are a way to skirt these draconian laws. A pair of breeding rabbits can produce a number of young so keep them separated until you are ready for them to reproduce. Naming the parents is essential to keeping your cover; you will have to slaughter the babies quietly to avoid detection.

Dolly Freed in her book Possum Living gives an in-depth look at raising animals for meat; I highly recommend it for anyone interested. Rabbit meat tastes similar to chicken and is not an unpleasant meal. If you provide lots of greens to your animals they will be much healthier than anything you can purchase in the grocery store. Like chickens I recommend slaughtering several at one time and freezing them until you are ready to eat.

Curing and Tanning Hides

Should you decide to raise your own meat for food you may want to save the hides instead of discarding them. Hides can be tanned with or without the fur to make rugs, blankets, throws, clothing or other items.

Curing and tanning hides is a lengthy process but you have the satisfaction of knowing that you used every piece of the slaughtered animal that you possibly could; the hides are durable and if you keep the fur on them they can provide you with significant warmth in the winter.

There are a number of ways to cure and tan hides. Some use harmful chemicals and others are a simple as a long soak in Fels Naptha soap. I am including links to a variety of methods in the Resources section.

MEDICAL AND DENTAL CARE

P revention is the key to health on a shoestring. Watch what you eat and what you do. Do not expect to live to be 100 if you smoke cigarettes, pop pills and drink yourself to insensibility every night. While there are home remedies that can help you there is NOTHING as beneficial as prevention.

Eat healthy and drink a lot of water. Take a pinch of salt a few times a day before you drink a glass. Water is one thing that is easy to acquire, super cheap and can drastically improve your health. Read books by Dr. F. Batmanghelidj for more information concerning the benefits of drinking water.

THE BENEFIT OF REST

One thing that will help you to stay healthy is a lot of rest. Do not sacrifice sleep to get more accomplished and listen to your body when it says it is tired. If you feel an illness coming on lie down and rest as much as possible. One of the benefits of shoestring living is that you can afford to rest when needed without having to worry about some company firing you for taking off work and being sick. You can rest and work at home without dealing with an ignorant boss.

This is also very important when it comes to aches and pains. Pain is a signal that something is amiss in your system. Ignoring the pain of a stressed joint can lead to serious if not permanent damage. When you catch a pain early enough a few days of rest will be all you need to enable your body to heal itself.

FEVERS

Contrary to popular opinion fevers do not always need to be treated. I learned this from my doctor, who refused to recommend treatment for a low-grade fever except in younger children who were obviously uncomfortable. She said that a fever is the body's way of killing the germs that make us sick. To eliminate the fever is to allow the germs to run loose and make us more ill. She recommended treatment only when the fever was higher than 103F or when a child was obviously uncomfortable. Since learning this I rarely treat a fever in myself now and only treat them in my daughter when she is uncomfortable or it gets higher than 103F. For more information about fevers visit the link in the References section of this book.

MEDICAL CARE AND PRESCRIPTIONS

If you have a clinic available you may be able to go there and get prescriptions if you need them. Some health departments will provide this as well. You have other options if these are not available to you.

FLU SHOTS

I do not recommend flu shots for anyone. While some say that they help prevent illness when myself and my daughter have taken them we ended up getting ill much more often (and more severely) for about a year after the shot was taken. I have also researched the flu vaccine [23] and discovered that some of the ingredients include Thimerasol, Squalene and Formaldehyde. Do you really want to put that stuff in your body?

Read Do It Yourself Medicine by Ragnar Benson for an eye-opening method of getting prescription medication. This book is filled with information that I consider essential if you want to become responsible for your own health. Also visit the download page of the Hesperian foundation for access to a whole library of free ebooks concerning health. I especially recommend the two books Where There Is No Doctor and Where There Is No Dentist produced by the Hesperian Foundation at http://hesperian.org/books-and-resources/.

There are online pharmacies that do not require prescriptions - and sell their products for much, much less than we can buy them here in the United States. I used Freedom Pharmacy [24] for years to purchase birth control pills for a hormonal imbalance. It was either that or spend over $200 a year for a prescription that cost $75 a

---

23

http://www.associatedcontent.com/article/2339122/swine_flu_vaccine_is_it_poison.html?cat=5
24 http://www.freedom-pharmacy.com/

month to refill a generic. I spent about $85 at Freedom Pharmacy to acquire 6 months of the medicine I needed, which was not much more than I had been spending for a single month using traditional methods of acquiring medication here in the United States. Search for the term "online pharmacies" to locate more websites.

Reading labels will help you to save a fortune in over the counter medication. For instance, some dog flea shampoos contain the exact same ingredients and dosages of human lice shampoo. Instead of paying $10 for a small bottle of lice shampoo use these flea shampoos instead. This allows you to inexpensively treat for lice without having to worry about doing without. When my children were younger it seemed as if they were always coming home with lice so I saved a fortune!

ANTIBIOTICS AND ANTISEPTICS

Our frequent use of antibiotics is helping to create bacteria that are resistant to known treatment methods. Doctors now recommend the administration of antibiotics less and less to prevent this occurrence.

Instead of antiseptic soap wash hands thoroughly using plain hand soap and rinse well. The rinsing is essential to remove bacteria from the skin. Do not skimp on hand washing for this is the single best thing you can do to prevent illness in yourself and your family. Always wash your hands after you use the restroom, handle something dirty and before you even think about touching food. Keep a clean towel on hand to dry with and use a new towel any time you think the old one is dirty.

I personally do not use antibiotic ointments anymore; we keep a container of Bag Balm and use it for dry skin and any scrapes or sores that we get. I have seen Bag Balm heal a dog that was stabbed under her chin by a gasoline thief. She had a huge gaping hole under her tongue and the owner could not afford a vet so I filled the hole with Bag Balm daily. The dog recovered completely.

HOME REMEDIES

I am not a doctor so the normal disclaimers apply. Always verify that you are not allergic or that any natural remedies you try will not conflict with your doctor's advice. I am not responsible if you kill yourself; I am only reporting here what I use personally. What works for me may not work for you.

I am constantly on the lookout for old home remedy books. My favorite standby is titled Green Pharmacy by James A. Duke.

Jalapenos

We eat a lot of jalapenos and onions to maintain health and to assist when we feel an illness coming on. I put them in our foods, layer them on sandwiches, add them to salsa and eat them straight.

When I feel like I am coming down with something I mince up some jalapenos (or puree them if I have a blender available) and scoop them up using some nacho chips. I have been known to live on that for days and it greatly helps if you start the regimen early enough in the illness cycle.

I cook a lot with onions; sautéed onions are a delicious side dish to any meal and are exceptional as a topping on burgers and other hot sandwiches. Just cook them in a skillet with some butter until they are almost transparent and serve with your meal.

Cayenne Pepper and Honey

This is a remedy I learned from some old-timers: the husband had a heart condition that doctors said would kill him in months. They would take ground cayenne pepper (from the spice section of the local grocery) and add a couple of drops of water until they could form the pepper into a ball. They would place the ball on a spoon and pour a liberal dollop of pure honey over it before quickly swallowing it. The honey has antibacterial properties and coats the cayenne so that you can swallow it without burning your mouth and the cayenne is wonderful for heart conditions according to the old timers I knew. The man lived for about 10 years using that simple remedy--many years longer than the doctors ever dreamed.

I have cured strep throat at home using cayenne pepper. Take a cup of warm water and place 1/4 teaspoon of cayenne pepper into it. Mix well and gargle with this mixture. It will burn your throat but will help with the bacteria causing the infection. When you can swallow again start swallowing the cayenne pepper balls from the previous paragraph then add nacho chips dipped in jalapenos as your throat heals. When I did it I didn't miss a single day of work and didn't go to the doctor but felt better within a couple of days. I did this for about a week though to make sure I killed the bacteria.

Ginger "Tummy Tamer" Candy

This candy was created in desperation one weekend. My baby girl was so ill she couldn't keep anything down, not even the nausea medicines they sell over the counter. She was sick and getting sicker while I was growing more concerned.

Ginger is wonderful for upset stomachs but I was at a loss for how to actually get it inside of her. This recipe was the result of my brainstorming. It worked so well that Katie begs me to keep a batch on hand at all times for those times when her "belly needs taming."

Note: I use powdered ginger in this recipe because it is easily found in grocery stores and in my experiments was more palatable to children than using grated ginger.

- 2 cups sugar
- 1-1/4 cup Sweet Dreams tea (or other regular Chamomile tea)
- 1 Tbsp. powdered Ginger (from the spice section)

Mix all of the items in a heavy pot over medium heat and allow it to boil until it reaches the soft crack phase. Stir constantly while boiling to prevent sticking. To determine if the candy has achieved soft-crack phase, pour a spoonful of it into a cup of cold water - soft crack will look like strands when it hits the water. Those strands will hold together when you grab them with your fingers but will feel somewhat soft. Don't worry if you overcook it - it will still be useful, just a bit harder to work with.

When it is ready pour it into a well-buttered metal baking sheet. Any type of flexible metal pan will do but make sure it is flexible. I use a metal pizza pan personally. Spread it out into a thin layer, working quickly so that it does not cool before you have finished. Allow it to cool completely.

Twist the metal pan to remove the candy. Break it into small pieces and have the ill person to suck on as many pieces as they desire.

Dill Pickle Juice

We drink dill pickle juice as a tonic when the jar is empty and also drink it when we get diarrhea. I use it instead of the anti-diarrheal medications available over the counter. Just put about an inch in a glass and drink it down. More won't hurt you if you finish off the jar however!

There are other home remedies out there but we honestly don't use very many of them at all. We watch what we eat, drink lots of water, get plenty of rest and focus on prevention. The human body is an incredible machine and can heal itself wonderfully if we just treat it well and give it a chance.

DENTAL CARE

As with your health prevention is essential when it comes to keeping your teeth in good shape. Some like Dolly Freed believe that dentists do more harm than good on even damaged teeth and in some cases I believe she is right. Modern fillings are designed to fall out, forcing you to return to the dentist and have them replaced. It is much better if you can have them capped with some sort of metal or replaced entirely so that you only have a one-time expense.

You can brush your teeth for practically nothing by dipping a wet toothbrush into a small container of salt or baking soda; both of these items will not only clean your teeth but help with bacteria. Rinse well with water when you are finished.

I have flossed my teeth at times with thread but if your teeth are close together the thread will break. You can prevent this by using a double thickness of thread coated in beeswax. I generally just spring for cheap waxed floss instead. Don't skip flossing; it is amazing how much gunk can stick between your teeth!

You can gargle using a small amount of hydrogen peroxide. This was recommended by a dentist years ago and is safe as long as you don't swallow. I follow the gargle with a clean water rinse because I don't want to chance swallowing it but my dentist didn't mention this. When my teeth feel really dirty I wet my toothbrush with hydrogen peroxide before dipping it into the salt or baking soda. It works really well!

For more information on dental care download the free ebook titled Where There Is No Dentist provided by the Hesperian Foundation.

PERSONAL CARE

Most of the items you find in the personal care section of the store are completely unnecessary.

For basics all you need is a bar of soap and perhaps a bottle of shampoo. If you sweat grab a stick of inexpensive deodorant.

Here are a few tips to save money on this area:

DEODORANT

Shop for deodorant with coupons. You may be able to get it for less or even free on double coupon days.

Sprinkle baking soda or corn starch under your arms instead of using deodorant at all. This is an all-natural and frugal way to avoid the purchase of deodorant.

BODY POWDER

Check the ingredient list of popular body powders and you will discover that most of them contain corn starch. Instead of using corn starch and unwanted chemicals use plain corn starch instead. This is what parents used on babies before body powder was commercially available.

LOTION

Instead of lotion use a small amount of a healing salve like Bag Balm. You can also use olive oil or mineral oil. Keeping your body well-hydrated by drinking lots of water will help as well.

MOUTHWASH

Plain water works well as a simple mouthwash and is virtually free.

Add a teaspoon of salt to a cup of warm water for a mouth rinse that will help disinfect your mouth and gums.

Make a rinse using half water and half hydrogen peroxide for an antibacterial mouth rinse. You may want to follow up with a plain water rinse as this may foam.

A dentist recommended rinsing with straight hydrogen peroxide, taking care not to swallow. This foams a lot so you may want to rinse with plain water when you are done. This was recommended for those with gum infections.

PERFUME

Instead of buying perfume take fragrant flowers from your yard and heat the blossoms in a small amount of olive oil. After a time the oil will absorb the floral scent, which you can dab upon your pulse points for a natural perfume.

You can also simmer the flower petals in water then strain through cheesecloth. I have included a link to instructions in the References section.

You can also purchase fragrance oil at the store; Wal-Mart sells large bottles for around $5; just dab this oil on your pulse points. I rub a little on my palms and then rub my hands through my hair to lightly add a pleasant scent. I get a lot of compliments from that!

Shampoo

Place a teaspoon of baking soda into a cup of warm water. Pour this over damp hair, rubbing in well. Scrub your head and then rinse with plain water. In my experience this works just as well if not better than store-bought shampoo and costs less than a penny per use; the only downside is that it does not lather like regular shampoos so some may not find this method enjoyable.

You can also clean your hair using oatmeal or corn starch: rub one of these items into your scalp and then brush out using a hairbrush. This soaks up the oils that make your hair appear dirty and is a great way to avoid washing your hair in the winter months.

Hair Care

There are two cheap methods to style your hair: keep it shaved or let it grow. I let mine grow though once I shaved it in sympathy for my cousin[25] and actually enjoyed the change. It itched and looked ragged when it first started growing back.

Some advantages to shaving your head are the fact that you will no longer have to brush and style it. You will also no longer need to purchase shampoo. Just rub some body soap on it and rinse well. This also works if you have short hair. I use this method whenever I have short hair.

For those who wish to grow their hair out there are a variety of places online to teach you how to keep it trimmed up. I just turn my head upside down after washing and give the ends a quick clip to keep them even. I saw the method on a television show (on dry hair); these women paid a fortune to hang upside down in a special frame so that a stylist could cut their hair in this "California" style. I just do it for free. When it is really long I bend over on a bed or on a sturdy table to keep my hair off the floor but I usually don't let my hair get that long.

There is a blog dedicated to instructions for self-trims. You can find it at http://feyeselftrim.livejournal.com/.

If you let your hair grow long you have a variety of ways that you can wear it. Some prefer just letting it hang loose while others braid or otherwise put their hair up. When I'm working around the house I keep it up in a bun or twist it up and hold it with a clip; sometimes I put it in a French braid for variety. I rarely do pony

---

[25] http://annienygma.com/2009/07/love-shave-for-my-cousin/

tails--when paired with a tee shirt and jeans they scream that you are either young or just lazy.

You can easily clean your hair using a cup of water and a tablespoon of baking soda: wet your hair and then pour the solution upon your head. Scrub well and rinse. You will be amazed at the amount of dirt this will remove!

If desired you can follow this with a vinegar rinse but after trying it both ways I didn't notice enough of a difference to bother.

I liked this method of washing hair but I eventually stopped because I missed the lather of traditional shampoos. I still do it on occasion though.

TOOTHPASTE

Dampen a toothbrush and then dip into some salt or baking soda. Brush your teeth and then rinse your mouth well. For extra cleansing power, dampen the toothbrush in hydrogen peroxide instead of water.

MOUTHWASH

Plain water works well as a simple mouthwash and is virtually free.

Add a teaspoon of salt to a cup of warm water for a mouth rinse that will help disinfect your teeth and gums.

Make a rinse using half water and half hydrogen peroxide for an antibacterial mouth rinse. You may want to follow up with a plain water rinse as this may foam.

A dentist recommended rinsing with straight hydrogen peroxide, taking care not to swallow. This foams a lot so you may want to rinse with plain water when you are done. This was recommended for those with gum infections.

TOOTHPICKS AND TOOTHBRUSHES

A twig from a sassafras tree makes an excellent toothpick. It's antibacterial action is great for plaque and bacteria that gets trapped within your teeth. These twigs were used in the past before toothbrushes were invented. Users would chew on one end of the twig and then take the frayed end and rub it up and down on their teeth to clean them.

Home Care and Cleaning

O ur home is not only our biggest expense but is also a huge time and money suck. We purchase expensive cleaners and spend our days off using them to clean and tidy our home.

One of the biggest things you can do to decrease the time and money you spend cleaning is to live with less. Declutter and eliminate the excess so that you can free up your space for what is important.

After you have finished decluttering you can make some inexpensive cleaners and start saving some serious cash.

Minimalist Window Cleaner
Dampen a microfiber cloth with warm water and scrub the dirty window. Rinse with clean water if extremely dirty. Dry the window using a dry microfiber cloth.

Basic All-Purpose Cleaner
In the days of our grandparents most commercial cleaners did not exist. One cleaner did and was used for almost anything: soap and water.

Grab a bar of soap. Some soaps you can use are:

- **Ivory**. This was what made the famous Ivory flakes our ancestors cleaned with. Proctor and Gamble grated up Ivory soap and marketed it in boxes for everything from cleaning laundry to washing floors.
- **Lye**. Lye soap was the standby of homes for ages. It was made by mixing lye with animal fat.
- **Fels Naptha**. Fels Naptha is a laundry soap that can also be used to clean really dirty items.
- **Octagon**. Octagon Soap can be used for laundry, dishwashing or general cleaning.
- **Zote**. This soap comes in several colors and can be used for laundry, dishes and general cleaning as well.

There are other soaps out there but these are the most popular (and least expensive) options. Just lather up the item to be cleaned and rinse well. Octagon, Zote and Lye soap can all be used to wash dirty dishes, but Ivory leaves a film that will cause intestinal upset. I do not know if Fels Naptha is safe to use on dishes or not.

If you desire to use these soaps in washing machines simply grate them before using. A tablespoon should be sufficient to clean a small load.

Non-Rinsing Cleaner

Ammonia and water can be used as a powerful all-purpose cleaner. The beauty of this mix is that it requires no rinsing. In old times rugs were hung outside and cleaned with a solution of ammonia and water. Use 1 cup per gallon of warm water for a basic solution. Ammonia has a strong aroma so you may wish to keep a window open while you are using it.

Do not mix bleach with ammonia. A deadly gas will result.

LIQUID LAUNDRY DETERGENT

- 1 cup grated Fels Naptha, Octagon or Zote Soap
- 1/3 cup Borax
- 1/3 cup Washing Soda (Sodium Carbonate)
- 1 Gallon of Water
- Empty 1.5 gallon container (recommended, but a 1-gallon container will work)

Place a quart of water in a large stock pan (2 quart capacity or higher). Add the grated soap and simmer on medium heat until the soap flakes have completely dissolved. Add the Borax and Washing soda to the water. Stir well until the mixture achieves a syrupy consistency.

Add the remaining water to the empty 1.5 gallon container (only use half of the remaining water if using a 1 gallon container).

Remove the soap mixture from the heat and pour into the container. Cap tightly and shake well. If using a 1 gallon container, pour in the remaining water but leave a 1-inch space at the top to allow for shaking.

To use, shake well and add 1/2 to 3/4 of a cup per load of wash. Use more for large or extremely dirty loads. This does not lather much so it is safe for HE washers.

For more cleaning recipes check out my book <u>The Minimalist Cleaning Method</u>[26]. The link is available in the References section.

---

[26] http://www.smashwords.com/books/view/35019

CONCLUSION

There you have it folks: the tips, tricks, recipes and links I use to live on a shoestring. I've tried to achieve a balance of providing you with the information you need while not boring you to tears.

I am a living example of how one can live well for very little; when we moved here all we possessed fit into our 1999 Ford van.

We started out with very little and ended up with more than enough. Here are a couple of photos:

The living room with my futon ready for business.

With the exception of the coffee table and futon in the above picture all of the big stuff was acquired after we moved in. The aquarium and stand were exchanged for computer work while the rest of the items were free.

It is my desire to give hope to those who feel as if they are financially drowning or who want the freedom to chase their dreams. You don't have to have thousands of dollars coming in every month to live like royalty; instead you just have to know how to use what you DO have!

Don't worry about what your friends and family will say; they will understand in time. Your true friends may not understand but they will support you nonetheless. If they don't support you then you know they weren't real friends to begin with. The peace and security you gain will far exceed any grief anyone will give you!

If there is anything you would like to see included in future editions of this book please email me at annie@annienygma.com.

Peace,

Annie

ABOUT THE AUTHOR

Annie Brewer is a frugal living expert who combines minimalism with frugality to live the life of her dreams. She has been writing since she was old enough to put pencil to paper and started living on a shoestring when she left her husband around 2001. Her mastery of the subject enables her to live on her writing income so that she can be a stay-at-home single mother for her youngest child.

She currently resides in Central Kentucky with her daughter and a menagerie of pets. Her days are spent writing books, working on her blog at http://annienygma.com, reading copiously and chatting online with Kessie, her dear friend of 28 years and counting.

Annie Brewer

It is her desire to help others through the written word. If this book has benefited you in any way she asks that you tweet, email or Facebook her to say hi.

CONNECT WITH ANNIE ONLINE:

Twitter: http://www.twitter.com/annienygma

Facebook: http://www.facebook.com/annienygma

Website: http://annienygma.com

Yahoo! Contributor Network:
http://contributor.yahoo.com/user/annienygma

Smashwords:
http://www.smashwords.com/profile/view/annienygma

Email: annie@annienygma.com

REFERENCES AND RECOMMENDATIONS

Adverse Possession:

http://www.foxnews.com/politics/2011/07/21/texas-mans-16-
property-seizure-throws-obscure-law-into-
spotlight/?test=latestnews

Alarm Clock Program (free download):

http://download.cnet.com/Free-Alarm-Clock/3000-2350_4-
75328290.html?tag=rb_content;contentBody

Car Living:

http://carliving.info/

Cheap RV Living (covers van dwelling):

http://cheaprvliving.com/

Curing and Tanning Animal Hides:

http://www.state.tn.us/twra/pdfs/tanninghides.pdf (right-click this
link and choose "save as" to save the PDF to your computer)
http://www.ehow.com/list_5946062_uses-fells-naptha-
soap.htmlhttp://www.ehow.com/list_5946062_uses-fells-naptha-
soap.html
http://www.soapsgonebuy.com/category_s/8.htm

Fax Online for free or low-cost (depends on file size):

http://www.faxzero.com

Feather Pillows and Mattresses:

http://www.associatedcontent.com/article/5501486/how_to_make_
homemade_feather_pillows.html?cat=24

http://www.associatedcontent.com/article/5526934/how_to_make_
an_american_futon.html?cat=24

Fevers:

http://www.nlm.nih.gov/medlineplus/ency/article/003090.htm

**Flu vaccine article (focuses on swine flu but the ingredients
are almost identical to regular flu vaccines):**

http://www.associatedcontent.com/article/2339122/swine_flu_vacc
ine_is_it_poison.html?cat=5

The **Foxfire series of books** is an excellent reference for all sorts
of older crafts. There are 6 books in the series and if you are
unable to locate them in used book stores search online for PDF
copies.

Free ebooks:

http://www.gutenberg.org/

http://gutenberg.net.au/

http://books.google.com/

http://www.archive.org/index.php

http://sacred-texts.com/.

http://www.free-ebooks.net/

http://www.manybooks.net/

Free Computer Operating Systems:

http://www.ubuntu.com

http://fedoraproject.org/

http://damnsmalllinux.org/

http://www.puppylinux.com/

http://www.opensuse.org/en/

http://www.linuxmint.com/

http://distrowatch.com/

http://bsd.org/

Free Music Downloads

http://www.yourfreemusicdownloads.com/

http://www.ez-tracks.com/

Free Software:

http://download.cnet.com/windows/

Freedom Pharmacy (inexpensive prescription medications without a prescription):

http://freedom-pharmacy.com/

Hesperian Foundation (free ebooks and materials on health and preventative medicine):

http://hesperian.org/

Homeless On Wheels

http://homelessonwheels.wordpress.com/

"How to Start Out or Over on a Shoestring" by Annie Jean Brewer

http://www.smashwords.com/books/view/69709

"How to Survive on Practically Nothing" by Edward H. Romney

"How to Survive Without a Salary" by James Long

"How to Write and Sell an Ebook" by Annie Jean Brewer

http://www.smashwords.com/books/view/36647

Internet Radio Stations:

http://www.shoutcast.com/

http://www.iheart.com/

http://www.pandora.com

http://www.live365.com/index.live

http://aolradio.slacker.com/

Kiddie Pool Gardens:

http://www.technologyforthepoor.com/UrbanAgriculture/Garden.ht
m

Live on a Boat

http://www.weliveonaboat.com/

Mail Remailer

http://www.usa2me.com/

Perfume:

http://planetgreen.discovery.com/fashion-beauty/perfume-garden-
flowers.html

http://www.bio-byte.com/articles/MakePerfume_01.shtml

Annie Brewer

"Poor Richard's Almanack" by Richard Saunders (Benjamin Franklin)

"Possum Living" by Dolly Freed

What happened to Dolly Freed:

http://www.paige-williams.com/

Potato Growing:

http://www.poconogardening.com/potato.html

http://gardendesk.blogspot.com/2008/10/garbage-can-potato-harvested.html

"Simplicity: Simply the Best Home Decorating book" Excellent resource for instructions to make curtains, throws, covers and all sorts of other home decorating items.

Simply Car-Free by Tammy Strobel: A Review

http://www.associatedcontent.com/article/5756060/simply_carfree_how_to_pedal_toward.html?cat=38

Software for Microsoft Windows and Apple Mac computers (very inexpensive):

http://www.waysale.com/softwares

Spartan Student (lived in a van while he attended college)
http://spartanstudent.blogspot.com/

Square Foot Gardening:
http://www.journeytoforever.org/garden_sqft.html

"The Autobiography of Benjamin Franklin" by Benjamin Franklin

"The Minimalist Cleaning Method" by Annie Brewer
http://www.smashwords.com/books/view/35019

"The Underground Guide to Living Frugal" by Bjorn Karger

"The Way to Wealth" by Benjamin Franklin

Three Sister's Garden:
http://www.nativetech.org/cornhusk/threesisters.html
http://faq.gardenweb.com/faq/lists/teach/2003045238014436.html

"Walden" by Henry David Thoreau

Video Websites:

Note: Some of these websites change frequently; if one goes down go to Google and search for the term "watch movies online." Never put your credit card or any personal information in, and never download a special program to watch them. If you have Windows Media player and VLC media player you are good to go.

http://1channel.ch

http://www.ovguide.com

http://www.hulu.com

VLC media Player:

Note: This is the official website link. You should never have to pay for this program.

http://www.videolan.org/vlc/

Waysale.com Software (inexpensive software):

http://www.waysale.com/softwares

"Where There Is No Dentist"

http://hesperian.org/publications_download.php

"Where There is No Doctor" and other free health-related ebooks

http://hesperian.org/publications_download.php

"Where to Work Online" by Annie Brewer

http://www.smashwords.com/books/view/36433

INDEX

Annie Brewer

Zote, 116

www.ingramcontent.com/pod-product-compliance
Lightning Source LLC
Chambersburg PA
CBHW070022300526
45794CB00001B/392